215G

V 4 -

ACADEMIA REVISITED

ACADEMIA REVISITED

a novel by
Lucien St. André

The Florham Park Press, Inc.
12 Leslie Avenue
P. O. Box 303
Florham Park, NJ 07932-0303

ISBN 0-912598-58-1

The central characters in this novel are fictitious. Minor characters were either invented by the author or were real people assigned to fictional roles.

Gratefully, I acknowledge the help and encouragement I received on this project from my friends, Stanley Strand and Charles and Bernice Weiss.

The author

ONE

Your soul to Satan sell.
Thereafter, serve him well,
And some day you will dwell
In the coolest spot in hell.

Henry sat alone at his table in the banquet room on the second floor of the Afton Restaurant, impatiently awaiting the arrival of his tardy host. The window table where he sat had been set for two. It overlooked the tarmac parking lot, beyond which the leaves of autumn celebrated that pleasant season in brilliant colors. He wondered why all the other tables in the room were bare until it occurred to him that it was probably a matter of privacy.

He had several other "whys" to consider, beginning with why Charles O'Malley, *wunderkind* of finance and real estate, wanted to confer with his old professor, and why here instead of in his office?

The last time he had seen Charles O'Malley, except on TV, was at his graduation from St. George's College about twenty-five years ago when O'Malley had picked up his diploma while Henry sat among his colleagues in that sauna called the auditorium, sweating until his academic robe was soaked with perspiration. Usually Henry remembered only his best students and those whom he had been forced to flunk. O'Malley fitted into neither category. Now, a quarter century later, this multi-millionaire financial genius had reserved the entire banquet room of a restaurant to entertain his old professor at lunch. Why?

A big man wearing a dark blue business suit was at the entrance. The *maître d'*? Henry adjusted his bifocals and his eyes and focused on him. No, it was Charles O'Malley. Somewhat bald, a little gray, but he'd know him anywhere. The same broad shoulders, the same erect, almost military carriage. The same handsome map-of-Dublin face, only a lot fuller now and beginning to wrinkle. And that arrogant bearing. Yes, he'd know him anywhere.

O'Malley's greeting was friendly. "Good to see you, Doc," he said as if he really meant it, extending his big hand. "It's been a long time. You're looking great, Doc. How are things?"

He could have said "Great for a man of your age," Henry thought.

In truth, the man O'Malley saw before him had aged fairly well. The darkly tanned face was thinner, its chisel-shaped chin emphasizing an oversized reddish nose, but the big floppy ears were still the same, ready to take to flight like Dumbo's. A slight slumping of his shoulders made a concession to his seventy years plus. But was he always this short? Maybe he shrank an inch or two as he got older. His hair, what there was of it, was the biggest difference, but he hadn't tried to hide its shrinkage under a rug.

He finally replied, "Yes, Mr. O'Malley, I'm retired now, you know."

"Yes, I know."

"I've been reading about you in the papers, Mr. O'Malley. For years now. Congratulations on your phenomenal success."

Two waiters materialized. One of them pulled out O'Malley's chair for him. The other filled their glasses with ice water and champagne. Both promptly left the room as if on cue.

"I've been reading about *you,* too, Doc, and it started me thinking. And I thought we should get together."

"You must be referring to the recent item in the local newspapers? The one that should never have been published."

"Yes. I know what you must be going through. Beggars by the hundreds. I know. I've been there. I'm *still* there. But I learned to adjust, and so will you."

Henry was having difficulty concealing his curiosity. But what's it to you? he thought. As if he were reading him mind, O'Malley said, "I think I can help you, Doc. Now you probably are thinking, 'Well, that's a switch. Most people want me to help them. But tell me about it'."

Henry took a sip of water; his throat needed it. "Well, Mr. O'Malley —"

"Chuck."

O'Malley raised his champagne glass (champagne this early in the day?). Following his example, Henry took a ceremonial sip, while he waited for Chuck to get down to business.

"The newspaper account was reasonably accurate, Chuck. A colleague of mine, in fact my best friend, recently — sort of died. He was a professor of economics and finance who lived a modest life while accumulating a lot of money in the stock market where most professors of economics and finance lose their shirts. In his will he left me in charge of a small foundation established by him 'to benefit mankind.' Its present net worth is about two and a half million dollars. I asked several of my colleagues for advice on how to spend this money. Obviously, one of them leaked the story to the press. Not that I blame him. It was too good a story. But the publicity that followed has made my life a nightmare."

Chuck nodded understandingly. "Yet, you must admit that the headline was irresistible for any newspaper editor. 'Professor to give away millions of dollars.' That grabs you. The first thing a reader would ask is 'How would any professor get millions of dollars to give away?'"

Henry was a little bit hurt but he was trying not to show it. After all, there *are* a few millionaire professors just as there are a few millionaire baseball players. Well there were many people wondering just how Chuck got his millions, including two congressional committees.

"Well, I hope you haven't already made up your mind, Doctor Boudreaux. I have something hot in the making that I think you'll like. If I can pull it off. And if it requires more money than you have, I'll help out. Helping people is part of my lifestyle. Of course, most of it never makes the headlines, which is the way I want it. I know what you must be going through. Crank telephone calls. Crank letters. People walking up to you on the parking lots of shopping centers, to say nothing about intrusive phone calls. People ringing your door bell. Beggars by the dozens. Everybody wants to be Queen for a Day."

"All of the above," Henry replied.

"Well, stand fast, Doc, and follow your own advice."

"My own advice?"

"Yes. You once said in one of your lectures which stuck in my memory that nobody was legally or morally obligated to answer an unsolicited letter. That we should do so only if it seemed to be to our advantage."

Henry nodded in agreement. It would take him weeks just to read the mail that had already come in. Appeals from organized charities on such expensive letterheads that they make you wonder. Pathetic begging letters, many of them scribbled in pencil. Also some obvious scams.

Preceded by the mouthwatering aroma of broiled steak, a waiter appeared.

"I took the liberty of ordering your steak rare," Chuck said. "If you want it medium or well done, don't hesitate to send it back."

This was a pleasant surprise. If Henry had placed his own order, he never would have ordered the most expensive item on the menu. He had too much pride. But it pleased him to get what he really wanted without having to appear greedy. Of course, O'Malley could afford it.

During lunch they discussed the economy while carefully avoiding mention of Chuck's financial empire. Henry let Charles do most of the talking; he didn't want to bring up topics that might prove embarrassing to his host.

The meal was a good one, the kind you would expect at the Afton, and the vintage burgundy was outstanding. Chuck did not come to the point again until he had picked up the check.

"Would you do this for me, Doc? I'm working on something I am sure you'll like. Don't make up your mind about what to do with that money until you talk to me again. It won't be more than another week or two."

"Why not?" Henry replied. He had no intention of rushing into anything anyway. Only young people rush into things.

Max met Henry at the front door, as Max always did. "Well, Max, what'll it be? Do I trust a man whom I don't really know any more? Ordinarily, I would not, but what motive could Charles O'Malley possibly have to be dishonest in this case? None that I can think of. Still there might be more here than meets the eye. What do you think?"

Max did not answer. Dogs don't talk, which is why they are such good listeners.

TWO

Gradually, Henry became aware of the annoying sound of music and awoke. Wasn't 5:30 an unnatural time for anybody to have to wake up? The alarm-clock radio would eventually shut itself off, so he could ignore it. Slowly, he reached for his bathrobe and covered his naked body with it. Grace was already half way to the bathroom, so he had to content himself with the basement powder room. Stepping carefully over his huge golden retriever who always insisted on sleeping in the bedroom doorway, he went downstairs. There he washed some of the sleep from his face with cold water.

In the kitchen he poured five tablespoons of decaffeinated coffee into the basket, four measured cups of cold water into the automatic coffee maker, and pressed the switch. A red light signaled that the brewing had begun.

As mindless as a robot, he filled two small glasses with reconstituted orange juice as the coffee machine started to perk. He brought one glass of orange juice to the bedroom where he left it on the dresser for Grace, and returned to the kitchen where he drank the other standing up, surrounded by the aroma of brewing coffee. Then he had his first cup of coffee. By the time Grace came into the kitchen in her light blue peignoir, he was fully awake.

"I've been thinking — " she began, then interrupted herself to take a sip of the aromatic coffee he had just poured into her cup, black, no sugar. He waited. She's putting on a few more pounds, he thought. She'd better watch it. But forty-two years of more or less happy married life had taught him when to keep his mouth shut. Thanks to her hair dresser, the gray of her hair had been recolored to a dark blonde, cut short, curled tightly. It occurred to him that neither old age nor the early hour had muted the beauty of that lovely Irish face. He took the four halves of buttered toasted English muffins from the toaster-oven, put two on each plate, and refilled their coffee mugs.

"What would motivate a man like the legendary Charles O'Malley to get involved in your project?" she asked.

Henry bit into his crunchy English muffin. He had been asking himself the same question. "He could be trying to improve his image. His financial empire is currently under investigation by two congressional committees as well as by state authorities, as I told you last night. He could use some good public relations."

"But why pick you?"

"Perhaps because he knew me when."

This statement was more for his own reassurance than hers.

Grace had finished her skimpy breakfast and begun to put on her make-up at the kitchen table, a habit which always annoyed Henry. He was still troubled about O'Malley's overture. It was all too pat. Too good to be true. Yet he knew he didn't dare reject it out of hand just because of his suspicions. Or was it paranoia? A man of such great influence would be a valuable ally in any event. If Henry's ideas were practical, if he were not the Don Quixote of higher education, he could indeed make a major contribution to the welfare of mankind by turning back the clock to better days, meaning days when he was young. When college teaching was a profession in the real sense of the word, and when research on a college campus was secondary to teaching.

While Grace was in their bedroom completing her toiletry and dressing for her job, Henry sopped up the coffee that had spilled onto the bare white formica table top. He prewashed the breakfast dishes under hot running water, then hid them in the dishwasher. Max, employing his one-sound vocabulary, reminded his master that he had not yet been fed and watered, so Henry filled his food and water dishes. Max chomped and slurped his satisfaction. Henry then trudged though the tiny dining area to the spacious living room centered around a large-screen television set. There he sank into his easy chair and waited for Bryant Gombel to narrate the news on Channel 4. A few minutes later Grace came into the living room. He helped her into her coat, kissed her goodbye at the front door, closed it behind her, and went back to bed.

Since his retirement from academia, Henry had assumed the role of house husband. He did all the housework. When Grace first went back to work their sons had been little boys, too young for kindergarten, and, since Henry was a convalescent at the time, he had taken over the duties of housekeeping. Later, when he began to teach full-time at St. George's College, they had divided the household chores. He became the cook, "since the French are better cooks than the Irish," and she did the cleaning. This was fine with her; she hated both cleaning and cooking. They had always divided the child care and their boys grew up, happy and well adjusted, mothered by both their mother and their father.

Many years later after Henry had retired from teaching, Grace kept her secretarial job at Allied so it was only fair that he should again pick up all the household chores, although he still hated cleaning. In addition, he had to keep the grass cut and a few flowers growing in the front yard, not to mention the vegetable garden in the back yard which meant so much to him. There was something primitively satisfying about harvesting super-fresh vegetables for you own table. Visitors often said to him, "You must love gardening."

He always replied, "I hate gardening, but I love gardens."

Henry was at the ShopRite supermarket in Eunice with his grocery list. Many of the shoppers were men, moving around, confused and confusing. He preferred to be surrounded by women shoppers; they knew what they were doing. They knew the etiquette of the supermarket. Usually, they did not double-park their carts while looking for an item in another aisle. Not like this inconsiderate bastard.

"Hello, Henry. How's retirement?"

The inconsiderate bastard moved his cart out the way of two unsmiling women. It was his friend, Raymon Donato.

"Hello, Ray. How's your retirement?"

"Not bad. And yours?"

"Not bad."

"Lousy!"

"Lousy!"

"But at least things are looking up for you, Henry."

"For me?"

"The two and a half million dollars, I mean. You have a good thing going there."

"Yes and no, Ray. It's a big responsibility. Let's not block the aisle. Say, Ray, let me buy you lunch. I have some beef stew in the freezer."

"If you made it, Henry, it's good. I'll bring the beer."

"Skip it. I've plenty of beer if you like Bud light."

At the check-out Ray dug into one pocket after another, muttering, "These damn coupons. I either forget them or I lose them."

"Don't knock them," his friend said; "They cut my grocery bill by twelve percent."

"**Good stew, Henry.** Good and hot, too."

Ray ought to know, thought his host. His wife, Angie, is a good cook and Ray, obviously, loved to eat.

"I grew those jalapiño peppers last summer, Ray. They've been in the freezer ever since. Since Grace doesn't eat stew and she doesn't like hot peppers, I — "

"You save them for your Dago friends like me."

"I never thought of it that way, but I guess you're right."

"But what was it you wanted to discuss with me?"

"I need your advice, Ray. Joseph White has saddled me with a big responsibility. The charter of his little foundation, which I now control, calls for his money to be used to improve the lot of mankind. That's a big order, a big responsibility."

"Then why don't you just divide the money among organized charities and be done with it?"

"Because if that's what Joseph had wanted, he would have done so himself. No. Joseph didn't think much of most organized charities. Too much organization and too little charity, he used to say. Well, one day we were discussing this matter and I said that if I had a million dollars I could change the face of the earth."

" 'Nonsense, Henry,' he said. 'You might do some good, but not that much.'

" 'Don't forget the multiplier principle,' I said. 'Get something good going, and it could snowball into something really good. Like the March of Dimes, for instance.'

"Well, I couldn't convince him. He was so pessimistic.

Of course, that's understandable considering all the horrors he had been through."

"He was pessimistic, all right. And extremely shy. He never had anything to do with anybody. Except you. And your family. Why you, Henry? I've always wondered, why you?"

"Why not me? Even a Joseph White needs at least one friend. Why me? Why not me?"

Ray lifted his glass and filled his mouth with red wine.

"Dago red. Pretty good."

"Courtesy of the brothers Gallo," his host replied. "I put half a cup of it into the stew when it was cooking. As you know, Joseph had a number tattooed on his forearm."

"Yes, I know. Nazi business. Was he Jewish? I know that not all concentration camp victims were Jewish."

"I don't know if he was Jewish or not. I never asked him and he never told me."

Raymond was astonished. "Friend all those years, and he never told you?"

"That's why we were friend all those years. We never asked each other personal questions."

"But you shared your home with him, your family. You would have thought — "

Henry served black Creole coffee, but no dessert. Raymon commented that the coffee tasted a lot like espresso. They took their demitasses to his study and sipped them slowly. Ray saw what had once been a bedroom was now comfortably furnished with a studio couch lengthy enough to take naps on and an old easy chair that really should be reupholstered. It was a rocker that could be converted into a recliner by a hand lever. It fitted Henry's arthritic body perfectly. His friends understood that they were supposed to sit on the couch. The east wall of the room had two large windows which gave you the illusion of sitting in a huge goldfish bowl except when the heavy blue drapes were drawn. An entertainment center covered most of the opposite wall. It was deep enough to hold a stereo, two large speakers, and a moderately large-screen TV set hooked up to a VCR. The heavy long table which ran along the other inside wall held an IBM clone computer, a modem and a laser printer. Above it were built-in shelves full of books and office supplies. A small desk which had belonged to Henry Junior when he was a child was crammed into the corner, piled high with papers, mostly letters. Henry was not an orderly person.

"Tell me, Henry. Did Joseph die the victim of an accident, or was he a suicide?"

Henry hesitated, then said, "I think it was suicide. It happened in the detached garage of his cabin in the Poconos. There was an explosion followed by a fire. He was found in his car burned to a crisp ."

"That's the way the newspapers reported it," his friend said. "What makes you think it was a suicide?"

"You had to know Joseph. He carried a burden of guilt heavily on his shoulders. He had escaped being gassed and cremated by the Nazis, but millions of other people had not. That, I know, weighed heavily on his conscience. Then he died from carbon monoxide gas and was immediately cremated in his garage. Does that look like a coincidence to you?"

Ray looked into his face. "No. But why kill yourself in October, the most beautiful month of the year?"

"Because you are happy, involuntarily happy. And you feel you have no right to be happy. Not when other members of your family are dead."

THREE

Henry hated to shave, and, almost as much, he hated to brush his teeth. Perhaps it was his tender skin and the sore gums he attributed to old age. Funny how you can tell a man's age and a horse's age by their teeth. As a man grows older his gums recede pushing the teeth upward, while a horse's teeth wear down.

On the other hand, he loved to take hot showers so much that he usually took two a day, sometimes three. They washed away that sour old-folks body odor he hated so much. So he tied the three things together. He'd get out of the shower and immediately lather his face. Then, while waiting for the lather to set, he'd brush his teeth with the Interplak electric toothbrush recommended by his dentist. His arthritic fingers and wrists kept him from flossing. Finally, he'd scratch the annoying lather from his face with a Bic disposable razor and his stubble along with it. That way, it wasn't so bad.

The gathering of the Boudreauxs was, as Henry had expected, a tense occasion. Clearly, their two sons were unhappy. Pat, the younger, was finally earning enough as an actor to support himself in a modest way, although the bigger roles on Broadway still evaded him. He blamed this on his lack of money to subsidize himself while he acted in off-Broadway and summer stock productions which would have given him the experience and exposure he needed. He now had a one-room apartment on Waverly Place in Greenwich Village with four locks on his front door. This, his only luxury, meant that he no longer had to put up with incompatible roommates.

The brothers were awaiting their father in the living room. Junior was seated on the new green velvet couch; Pat had beaten him to their father's easy chair. The television set was pictureless and silent.

Pat was saying to Junior, "Typically, summer stock pays about a hundred and fifty dollars a week and a place to sleep. That means about a hundred after taxes, travel costs and union dues. The only way I could make ends meet is to live on peanut-butter sandwiches. And that doesn't take into account when I'm not working."

Henry Junior wanted to say "Why don't you give it up, Pat; it isn't worth it. Get a real job." But, knowing how this advice would be received, he restrained himself. Instead he commiserated.

"Yes, I know how you must feel."

"No, you don't," was Pat's bitter reply. "You can't possibly know how unfair it is. If your family has connections in the theater, it can pull strings to get you auditions and a good agent and that can be all-important. Or if they can afford to subsidize you. That way you can afford to act in summer stock for a hundred a week take-home pay."

"And if you get no help, what do you do?"

"I don't know. Being an actor is the only thing I ever wanted to be."

Pat was dark and good-looking, like his father, except that he was much taller. Some said that he, and not his brother, should have been baptized "Henry, Junior." In contrast, Henry Junior was fair of face. His eyes were steel blue. Except for his large nose, he was said to have been the very image of his grandfather, Patrick Murphy of the Boston Murphys. His full beard, blond streaked with gray, emphasized his prematurely balding, a fact which did not seem to bother him. Unlike the other Boudreauxs, he was overweight, a testament to the culinary skills of his wife, Inez.

Henry joined his sons in the living room. "Boys," he said, "I need your advice."

"A bit late for that, don't you think?" said Pat caustically.

Ignoring his brother's unkind remark, Junior asked, "About what, Dad?"

"'Uncle' Joseph's foundation. How do you think I should spend that money?"

"Well, I'm between shows," Patrick said. "Put me on your payroll and I'll devote full time advising you on that subject. And you could put Junior on part-time. I assume you also could use some money so you could put yourself on full-time at a good salary."

Junior said nothing. He, too, needed money badly. Having raised the down payment for the home he had just bought in

Florham Park by several smaller loans, he was sometimes late in making one or the other of his payments.

Finally, their father replied. "You miss the point. I am morally committed to operating this foundation as efficiently as possible. Unless you are willing to work as a file clerk at a file clerk's salary there's no place for either of you."

Pat got nasty. "You know, Dad, I can't understand you. You looked after Joseph White for all those years. You were the only friend that impossible man ever had that I know of. Who else would want to put up with his eccentricities? And what does he leave you and your family when he passes on? Not one penny. You call that a friend?"

"I call that a friend," his father patiently replied. "You see, several years ago when Joseph was even more depressed than usual, he seemed to be on the verge of suicide. He told me so. Then he said that he had made out a will naming me, my wife and my sons as his heirs because I had treated him like family. Like a brother. That was something to think about. What would a brother do in a situation like that one? Everything he could to save his brother's life, of course. So I told him that I did not want to be his heir. I advised him to make out another will, leaving his money to charity.

"Well, that's what did it. When Joseph learned that I'd rather have him alive than to have all his money, his attitude toward life changed. At least for a while. He set up the foundation and, following my advice, he wrote a new will leaving all his wealth to it."

The phone rang and Henry left to answer the kitchen extension. Patrick was shocked. "I don't believe it. I just don't believe it. Dad is so unrealistic. He gets a chance to become a millionaire and he blows it. To say nothing about what he did to me — and you. Professors are really stupid. Do you know what I could do with that much money?"

"Set up your own production company and star in your own play?" Junior suggested.

"Smart ass," his brother replied.

When Henry returned to the living room, his sons were silent. It seemed as if he had interrupted a conspiracy. "Just one more securities salesman," he said by way of explaining the phone call. "Now what was I saying?"

"You were saying that you threw away our legacy," Patrick said acrimoniously.

"Your *what?*

"Money your sons and your grandchildren should have had."

Henry could not contain his fury. "I did no such thing. In the first place, the money was not mine and if I had permitted Joseph to give it to us that would have, in all probability, cost him his life. I could never live with that on my conscience. And in the second place, who the hell ever told you that you are legally or morally entitled to a legacy?"

Pat had begun to regret his words; Junior was glad that he had remained silent. Henry continued.

"You both received a college education. Your tuition was paid. That was your legacy. If you worked part-time it was to pay for things you could have done without."

He calmed down a bit. "Traditions about inheritance go back to land-based economies. A young man had to inherit land if he were to support himself well. So it was a father's moral obligation to hold on to his land and pass it on to his heirs. Today, it is more important that our sons and daughters receive job-related training in their youth. This — "

"But we got tuition remission from St. George's; our education did not cost you a nickel," Pat said.

"Like hell it didn't. This fringe benefit persuaded me and others like me to teach for a smaller salary than that which we would otherwise have accepted."

Junior did not know how to respond. His father's arguments were logical, but he did not want to alienate his brother. So he said nothing.

Henry continued, "Savings were impossible on my small salary. My huge medical bills didn't help, either. So my children will have no cause to rejoice when I die, since I'm going to die broke. I have no assets to speak of except this house which is valuable because of a fluke in the economy. When your mother and I die, it will go toward the education of our grandchildren. If we are still alive when they are in college, we'll mortgage the house for them."

"You call that fair?" Patrick protested. "I have no children."

"Then get married and produce some," his father said.

Henry drew back the heavy drapes in his study and the morning sunshine rushed in to brighten his day. For a while, he gazed sadly over at the vegetable garden which he had abandoned to weeds for the winter. A pathetic sight. Evil's victory over Good.

He remembered he had several unpleasant jobs to do today. Which of these must he do immediately? Which could he postpone? Well, the carpet on the living room-dining room floor needed vacuuming badly. That's the trouble with golden retrievers; they constantly shed their long yellow hair. Meanwhile, he'd put the breakfast dishes in the dishwasher and, since it was now full, got it started.

Unpleasantly, his words with Pat yesterday came back to haunt him. Perhaps the "kid", who was over thirty years old, had a point. Why not use the money in the foundation to promote the arts, or, more specifically, to subsidize talented actors. Aye, there's the rub. Who would determine which talented young actors to subsidize? Himself? He couldn't possibly identify raw talent. Pat? Wouldn't he simply decide to give himself the biggest subsidy? Sincerely, too, since artists are necessarily egotists. Otherwise, they would not go into the arts.

What about that little man — it could have been a woman — who painted, painfully no doubt, such exquisite pictures on the walls of that cave in France fifteen thousand years ago? Why did he do it? Why was he so painstaking? Probably because he felt a compulsion to do so. Surely, no one paid him for his work. And why did Beethoven and Mozart work so hard for a pittance. Or Van Gogh for nothing? Probably for the same reason. Pat didn't just want to be an actor. He had to be an actor.

The dishwasher was humming, with an occasional click of plate against plate. He plugged in the vacuum cleaner and it roared, drowning out the voice of a newscaster. The golden dog hairs on the carpet were slowly, inexorably sucked into it.

Speaking of monetary remuneration, a well-known — now where was he? He had forgotten.

By the time he had finished vacuuming the living-room-dining-room, he had decided that he could not, in good conscience, use Joseph's money to subsidize Pat's career. It simply did not fit the definition of "for the benefit of mankind."

"A cup of coffee, Dad? Or could you call Mom and see if she would like to come over for dinner tonight? We have plenty."

He looked toward the stove, from which that tantalizing aroma of *polo en vino rojo* was drifting and wondered if the salivating he was trying so hard to conceal were visible. Grace did not eat Mexican food unless the recipe were gringoized by eliminating most of the hot spices. And even then, politely and reluctantly. He demurred.

Inez poured him a hot cup of coffee, another for herself and joined him at the kitchen table. How lovely is this classic Spanish beauty, he thought; if I had to select my own daughter-in-law, the way they did in the old days, I could not have made a better choice.

She looked up at him, her big brown eyes wide. "My husband tells me that you had a quarrel with Pat."

When speaking to her father-in-law, she always said, "my husband." She couldn't call him Henry, as she usually did, for that would be confusing, and she hated to call him "Junior."

Pat's outburst was exactly what Henry had dropped by to discuss with her. He nodded and waited.

"I can't really blame Pat," she said. "After all, what's that the poet said about a dream deferred?"

He waited for her to continue; she did. "On the other hand, I can't excuse him for being so rude to his father. A good father."

"Am I? Am I a good father? When should a man's devotion to his family end and his moral obligation to a sacred trust take priority?"

She knew he did not expect a reply. He rephrased it. "When does your obligation to your family take precedence to a moral commitment?"

She was still silent.

"You know, Inez, when we first moved to Eunice our street was a dead-end street. This was one of the reasons we bought where we did. The street behind us was on the blueprint as the one to cut through the park. Then the mayor's son bought a house on that street and the planning board changed its plans. It cut this street through instead, to the inconvenience of a hundred families over the past thirty years. No one doubted that the change was politically motivated. Yet some people commended the mayor for being such a good family man. I could not. I said he had abused his power and ignored his moral responsibilities."

"I think I see what you mean," she finally said as she rose to check on the chicken. "I agree with you. The mayor was morally wrong."

"Thanks, dear," he replied as he got up to leave. "Thanks a lot."

She wondered what he was really thanking her for.

FOUR

Henry still wondered if he had not gone too far in his commitment to his deceased friend at the expense of his family. Was it wrong to impose the personality of this strange man on his wife and sons all these years? He himself had never thought of the presence of Joseph as a hardship. The man had a keen mind and his conversation was stimulating, even when you did not agree with him, which was most of the time. Different, yet stimulating, or perhaps stimulating because it was different.

"Very good soup, Henry. My Angie couldn't have made it better. What's your secret ingredient?"

"Soup," Henry replied.

Ray frowned down at his empty soup bowl."

"Yes, it's not stew; it's soup, but what do you put in it to make it so good?"

"Specifically, Campbell's tomato soup. You see, Ray, I start off by boiling a piece of chuck with a bone in it. I start it in cold water. After an hour's simmering, I skim off the crud that comes to the surface. Then I add two cans of tomato soup and whatever vegetables I have in the garden or the refrigerator or the freezer. Such as beans, peas, carrots or sweet peppers or hot peppers, and certainly, chopped celery and onions. I simmer it for another hour and serve with Italian or French bread or crackers."

"I'll have to tell Angie."

"Better yet, why don't you surprise her with a hot pot of soup the next cold day?"

"Because I don't think she could stand the shock of me cooking a meal. Not to change the subject, or rather, to change the subject, have you made any progress in deciding how you are going to benefit mankind?"

"I got some interesting suggestions," Henry said. "Hundreds of them. Little things that matter. Such as the elimination of utility poles to improve safety. The elimination of foliage at street corners and on parking lots when it obscures visibility, outlawing window envelopes, especially those with an extra flap to hold extra advertising. Lobbying for a law making sales pitches by telephone illegal as an intrusion of our privacy. Or big things, such as housing for homeless families, soup kitchens to help feed them, health care for the poor.

"The only thing that bothers me is that the little things shouldn't have priority to Joseph's money, and the big things would require too much of my personal attention."

Henry rinsed off the two soup dishes in hot water until they were free of tomato sauce and grease and put them in the dishwasher.

The next day Henry, under Max's supervision, opened the door to Robert Chang.

"Glad you could come over, Bob. There's something I want to discuss with you."

"No problem, Henry. I wasn't doing anything in particular."

"A drink?"

"My usual."

With a scotch-on-the rocks in one hand and a Courvoisier in the other, the host led the way to his study where he handed the scotch to his friend.

"I ran across one appeal that touched me deeply, Bob. I want your reaction."

He took a sip of his cognac and continued. "This letter is from a political refugee. The English is poorly written, as you will see, but that makes it all the more eloquent. To summarize it, the writer states that he is a refugee from a tyrannical government, that someone rescued him and gave him a new life in America, and that was the best thing that could ever happen to him or anyone else in a similar situation. He believes that I could do nothing better with the money I have to spend than to enable worthy people to flee from tyranny and settle down in the land of opportunity.

"I thought that since you were once a political refugee you'd have an opinion on the subject."

Bob took another sip of the whiskey and replied, "I do." He paused. "As you know, in 1947 I was part of that seven hundred mile walk out of the heart of China. Along with thousands of other people displaced by the advance of the Communists, I walked the whole way, disguised as a coolie, pulling my wife and infant son in a rickshaw, with my two little boys walking beside me. I brought to this country with me a wife, three sons and a Harvard M.A. I received no help from the Chinese government, and no help from the American government. I had been an investment banker in China when Chiang Kai-shek was in control; I became a professor of philosophy at Farleigh Dickinson University."

He paused again, and his host found himself visualizing his friend and his family in an endless procession of people walking seven hundred miles.

"Henry, do you realize how many of the world's population live under tyrannical governments? At least two and a half billion people. That's ten times the present population of the United States. Let's assume that half of them want to come to this country. Can we let that many in without destroying the United States?"

"Obviously, no." Henry replied.

"Of course, we could let some of them in. But what criteria should we use to determine admission? Religion? No, that would discriminate against those of other religions. Ethnicity? No that would discriminate against other ethnic groups. Race? No, that would discriminate against other races. A quota system? No, in practice that would discriminate against almost everybody."

"What, then?" Henry asked.

"You asked me for an opinion, and this is it. Let in those people we need. Let in those people who would help this country, not those who simply needed to get in."

Henry agreed. "You'd think that after the indiscriminate admission of Cuban refugees, not all of whom were refugees, that we've learned a lesson. America's first priority should be

Americans. Right now, I understand, we need servants and agricultural laborers. OK. Open the gates to servants and agricultural workers."

Henry refilled their glasses and the conversation turned to another subject. He had already made up his mind; he would not touch the problem of refugees, not even with a ten-foot pole. He had never dreamed that it would be so difficult to give away money.

It had become a custom for Henry Junior to take his wife and children over to his father's house for brunch every Sunday after Mass. Henry Senior would drive over to Dunkin' Dohnuts in Madison every Sunday morning for a dozen assorted doughnuts, paid for in part with a coupon. Sometimes he stopped at Gruber's Bakery for sweet rolls, or a pecan ring. He liked pecans because they reminded him of his native Louisiana and the tall trees where every autumn he threw sticks into the branches to bring down the tasty nuts. He also tried to keep in mind the varied preferences of his family, but this was difficult since preferences frequently changed.

They would then loiter around. David, who was five, was inevitably at a television set, Hélène, nine, in constant motion. Junior read the two newspapers, while the two women talked, usually about the children. Even with the noise, or maybe because of it, Henry found these mornings so relaxing that he dreaded the possibility that his son would be transferred out of the area. He'd miss them terribly, especially David.

Henry had to go to the ShopRite supermarket. He wished he were the kind of efficient shopper who could buy a week's supply of groceries at a time. Every time he tried it, of course, there was something he'd forget or fail to anticipate. Max loved to come along for the ride. He would block the front door completely with his huge body to make sure he was not overlooked. During the ride he would nonchalantly observe the panorama they were passing. Henry drove a 1982 Dodge Omni. Its doors groaned loudly when he opened them, its front floorboard took in water when it rained, and half the time its fanbelt squeaked, complaining. But he loved it. It started without trouble on the coldest day, and its four-cylinder engine was peppy enough to leave bigger cars behind in an up-hill sprint. Short and narrow, it was easy to fit into a tight parking spot.

On the parking lot, Max would either sleep in the car or sit up in it so that passing shoppers could admire his great size and his beauty. That day Henry had just pulled into a parking space, one selected because it permitted him to drive out rather than oblige him to back out. Arthritics can back out, but it is painful and Henry was no masochist. Since Max was in the back seat, Henry had left all windows partly open. Nobody would try to steal a car with such a monster as Max in it.

"Say, Mr. Boudreaux. Don't you answer your mail?"

It was Ernest Hause, who lived two blocks down the street from him. Henry hated to be called by anything but his first name by his neighbors. He also hated to be called "mister" by someone who knew his proper titles were "professor" and "doctor."

Ernie knew this, and why he persisted in doing otherwise was a mystery to Henry.

"Not recently, Ernie. I have a backlog of letters so big it will take me months to get through all of it."

Ernie paused. "It may be too late by that time."

"What do you mean?"

"Well, if you had read my letter — " his tone was accusative — "you'd know that my grandson has leukemia. His doctors have given up on him. Our only hope is a new treatment that we can get only in Switzerland. I saw that on TV. Well, it'll take about fifty thousand dollars to get him over there and pay for his treatment. I thought that if you knew about it you'd want to help. What better thing can you do with that money you inherited than save a child's life?"

It took a while for Henry to answer. "I don't know, Ernie. It's an unfair question to begin with. It implies that I have a responsibility to this child."

"You might be able to save his life."

"And again I might not be able to save his life. And we're back to the question of responsibility. Well, all I can tell you is that if we decide to use the money for medical purposes, I'll make sure that your grandson will be one of the first persons considered."

Clearly Ernest had hoped for more, but he didn't press the point.

Ernie had a lean and hungry look, and Henry wondered if his wife fed him well; she certainly looked well fed herself. He thought of them as Jack Sprat and his wife.

Several days later Henry was discussing the matter with both Raymon Donato and Gerald Walton over lunch at the Afton.

"I don't like it," Ray said. "The man saddles you with an obligation that is not yours. He has no right to do that. Ask yourself if you are afraid of him or your conscience."

Henry shrugged his shoulders.

Gerald wanted to know if Ernie were a friend.

"Hardly," Henry replied, "although I've known him for many years. He used to be my milkman."

"Your milkman? I haven't heard that word in years."

"He used to put a quart of milk on my porch every morning and collect for it at the end of every month. It's one of those conveniences that have since faded away. But he never was a friend. You see his wife thought that a three-thousand-dollar-a-year college professor was socially inferior to a six-thousand-dollar-a-year milkman and she snubbed my wife."

"You know, I've always wondered whatever happened to milkmen," Ray remarked.

"Social change," Gerald replied. "You know, years ago I never begrudged the milkman his hard-earned money. He really earned it. He had to get up around three o'clock every morning, seven days a week, drive in all kinds of weather."

Ray agreed. "But those guys wanted it both ways. They wanted a better lifestyle, but when they got it they still wanted to be compensated for hardships they no longer suffered.

"Their first step was to deliver milk only every other day. This meant that they could get up later and still complete their rounds. It also meant that their customers had to have on hand more milk than they wanted. Then the milkmen wanted — and got — Sundays off. This made the milk business a lucrative target for the jug stores. Eventually, home delivery became so unprofitable that it was abandoned."

"And what happened to Ernie?" Gerald asked.

"He went to work for United Parcels," Henry replied.

"Still a well-paid job."

"Yes, but not the aristocrat of labor that a milkman was. I don't think Ernie ever adjusted to that fact. He spent his life engaged in conspicuous consumption. Trips to Bermuda. Cadillacs."

"And now he wants you to pay for his extravagances?" asked Ray.

"Seems like it."

"What's worse, he seems to think you're obligated to do so," Gerald said.

Finally Ray said, "Look at it this way, Henry. If you go through that neglected mail of yours you will probably find twenty or thirty equally serious cases of sick people begging for help. All the money you have at your disposal probably wouldn't cover the cost of helping half of them. Is it fair that you should discriminate against half your requests in favor of the other half. What would be the basis of your discrimination? Do you draw straws? Should human life be reduced to a gamble where the lucky live and the unlucky die? No, Henry, you can't play God. Back off."

FIVE

At 8:20 Henry arose. This time he was fully awake. He remembered that he had a lot of work to do. First, he would sound out a few of his retired colleagues. Perhaps a fifth or sixth opinion might put his mind at ease. He was in the bathroom with lather on his face, naturally, when the doorbell rang. Evidently the uniformed messenger was used to getting dirty looks in the early morning. He ignored Henry's as he handed him the heavy brown envelope from Charles O'Malley. It contained such a thick package of documents that Henry began to dread the commitment he was considering. And he was supposed to be retired? Retirement? He had a strange feeling that his retirement was coming to an end.

The envelope contained about a hundred sheets of paper, mostly photocopies of handwritten notes, or so it seemed. On top was a single small sheet of expensive-looking bond paper with O'Malley's letterhead stamped on it in gold. Impressive.

November 17, 1989

Dear Doc,
  You probably know by now that the good brothers
  have already closed down St. George's College.
  They wanted me to bail them out again, but I
  refused because, in my opinion, old St. George's is
  no longer viable. I do believe, however, that you
  and a few of your retired colleagues could start a
  new college on that campus and develop it into
  something really good. I've been on the Board of
  Trustees of St. George's long enough to know that
  two and a half million dollars is just enough to get
  you started, but I intend to help you prove your
  point — that the best and the most economical
  road to a liberal education is through the small
  liberal arts college.

It was signed "Chuck."

The idea was irresistible. Why hadn't he thought of it?
Because he did not have enough money to start a college, of
course. The cost of the land and buildings for a college would
be much more than two and a half million dollars. Only with
the backing of a sympathetic financial institution such as
O'Malley's letter implied could he even start. Henry certainly
had not been thinking in such grandiose terms. Joseph, what
are you getting me into? His mind went back to the time he
first met Joseph White. Yes, it was his second semester at St.

George's, early in January of 1954. That had to be it. He had been teaching there for one semester already, and it was Joseph's first. Speaking with a thick German accent, he seemed to be very self-conscious. It was soon apparent to Henry that he was trying to find his way around the campus while avoiding the embarrassment of asking directions.

So Henry volunteered. He could not help but notice the deep red scar on Joseph's throat, but did not mention it. Joseph saw the burn scars on Henry's hands and neck but did not mention them.

"I had a burn accident the year before last," Henry volunteered.

Joseph volunteered nothing.

"I could use a cup of coffee," Henry said. "Would you care to join me?"

Then he regretted his invitation; clearly, it made his new acquaintance uncomfortable. The words they exchanged at the table in the school cafeteria could hardly be called conversation, with each man respecting the reticence of the other. They did learn, however, that they were both teaching in the Department of Economics.

"This is only my second semester here, but if I can help you get settled, just say so," Henry said. The next cup of coffee they had together was in Henry's home, which was only five blocks away. There were many others to follow.

It was several months later when they were having lunch in St. George's cafeteria between classes. Two other teachers had invited themselves to share their table, briefly interrupting their conversation. Joseph was saying, "As I was telling you, my dear, this situation — "

To his confusion, he was interrupted when the two started to whistle.

"Excuse me, Joseph," Henry explained. "In America such phrases as 'my dear' on the part of men are restricted to women. I mean, we do not speak to our male friends in endearing terms but in insults."

"Insults? I do not understand."

"Yes, insults. Now in Germany it is correct to address your friend as *mein lieber. Nich wahr?*

Natürlich.

"And in France a man calls his friend, 'mon cher'. *N'est pas?*"

"*Mais certainment.*

"Well, in this country you don't. You call him 'you old bastard' or 'you old son-of-a-bitch', and if you still have all of your teeth, you know he is a close friend."

Impossible, Joseph must have thought, but he saw the other two teachers nodding, so it must be so.

"**Oh boy, what's that I smell?**" Robert Chang stood in the front doorway, a broad grin on his handsome round face. Not long ago when Henry had remarked that his hair was slow in turning gray, Robert had said that the Chinese did not get gray. "We go from black hair to white hair almost overnight."

His hair now had the dignity of being white. Max recognized him as a friend, and the golden retriever returned to his favorite corner of the carpet to resume his nap. It seemed to Henry that as his dog got older he was always sleeping. Perhaps it was the daily dose of phenol barb which his vet had prescribed. Max was an epileptic.

"Come on in, Bob," Henry called out as he continued to stir the chicken in the glass casserole dish before returning it to the microwave oven. The Hitachi rice cooker rang a bell to say that the long-grain rice was fully cooked. Henry lifted the top, and stirred the contents with a fork, leaving it set on "warm."

"Sit down, Bob. Over here."

He poured his guest a glass of Glen Ellen chablis.

"Did you cook the chicken or Grace?" his friend inquired.

"You know what you always say, Bob. If a man wants a really good meal, he cooks it himself."

They laughed.

The microwave buzzed its notice, and Henry carefully removed the casserole to the kitchen table. Bob was too close a friend to be considered "company" so he could serve himself directly from the rice cooker.

"Good chicken," Bob said, "but I think Grace makes it better."

His friend grinned at his humor. "Perhaps you're right."

After a while Henry came to the point. "I want your advice, Bob. You know how we used to talk about the waste of money by university bureaucracies and the economies that small colleges could make if they stopped trying to act like large universities?"

"Yes."

"Well, now I have a chance to prove my point. I can have my own liberal arts college. If that is what I want."

"And I thought you wanted my advice on how to spend the money that Joe White — "

"Joseph White. He did not like to be called Joe. Yes, that

too. You see, they overlap."

Bob took a sip of the chilled white wine and waited as Henry continued. "Yes. Charles O'Malley wants to help me buy St. George's buildings and grounds and reopen it as a no-frills institution."

"No frills, hun? And what frills would you eliminate? Football?"

"St. George's never had a football team. The new institution would not have a basketball or baseball team, either. Not even track. No varsity athletics at all."

"And those kids who wanted varsity athletics — "

"Could still go to Seton Hall or Farleigh Dickerson. Our target market — "

"Our?"

"I was hoping you'd come out of retirement and help me get this thing started."

Bob was silent. Then he said, "Sounds good to me. I'm bored with retirement anyway."

"I'm hoping that a few more of the good ole boys will feel the same way. We already have a campus and buildings. Now all we need is a faculty and student body."

"And an administration," Chang added.

"No administration," Henry said.

"No administration?"

Henry smiled. "The whole idea is to have no separate administration. The full professors will constitute the Board of Trustees. From these a president, a vice president, a bursar, a dean, etc., will be chosen to fill the individual positions. Each of these will also teach. We can save a lot of money that way."

Ignoring the mess they had created in the kitchen, they went to Henry's study. Two large cartons of unopened letters stood on the tiny desk. Pointing to them, Henry said to Robert, "That's what happened when word got around that I had millions of dollars to give away. About a third of what I've sampled comes from professional money raisers for organized charities. I guess these people subscribe to clipping services and write to every prospect who turns up."

Robert sat on the squeaky secretary's chair at the little desk and Henry handed him the large, thick envelope.

"These are the papers Chuck sent me."

"So it's Chuck now, is it?"

Henry smiled and went on. "He saved these notes from his student days. More than twenty-five years ago. Can you imagine that?"

The memo from Chuck was on top. Obviously what Bob had here were photocopies of notes that Chuck had taken of Henry's lectures. Some of the more salient points had been underscored with a red felt tip pen. When Bob read these passages, Henry's ideas of a quarter century ago as interpreted and edited by one of his students. He wondered how they would hold up in the world of today.

Bob read one example out loud.

> "Summer school is a watered-down version of the fall and spring semesters; a third semester extending through the summer would be a far better use of resources. It would permit a good student to get his B.A. in less than three years."

"Well, I have not changed *that* opinion," Henry said. "Two years and eight months of liberal arts for a B.A., followed by two years of graduate school for an M.A. or an M.B.A."

Henry anticipated Bob's objection. "Pre-med students and science majors, of course, would not fit in. Neither would engineering majors. Let them go to a college which follows the traditional patterns. But the vast majority of college students could fit into the new pattern very nicely. What I have in mind is not just time, but quality time. I have seen far too many under-graduates leave the campus at noon to rush to a full-time job."

Robert nodded in agreement and Henry continued. "Bad enough when they had to do it to pay tuition and living expenses. Absurd when they did it to pay for a new car, or even to start a family. What these people want is a degree, not an education. Maybe that is still true about the majority of college students today, but the new version of St. George's — which I would call Santa Sophia — would not want such so-called students."

Henry's enthusiasm took over. "We would cater to the kind of person who wants total immersion in his or her studies with a minimum of distractions. Those who really wanted to learn."

Robert flipped over a few pages and read out loud. "Colleges should not be in the hotel business. They're very poor at it."

"Still true," Henry injected. "Dormitory life is supposed to encourage study. Very often it does just the opposite. Serious students often have to do their homework in the library because the distractions in the dorms interfere with their concentration. Roommates are often incompatible, sharing so few common interests that conversation is reduced to small talk. As for the food, they might as well be in a hospital."

"Yes, I agree," Bob replied. "In many schools the vast majority of the students are day-hops, which means practically no dialogue outside classes. Athletics and extra-curricular activities are monopolized by the ten percent of the students who remain on campus all day. Team projects would mandate our students' interaction and reaction. No varsity sport. In Europe there is no such thing. Intramural sports for all who want them. No salaried coaches. Leave that to other institutions."

"What about tuition?" Robert asked.

"Tuition? I believe we can balance our budget on half what the private universities charge. Roughly that's seventy-two hundred a year, or thirty-six hundred dollars a semester. I'd start by charging eighteen hundred dollars a semester. I'd also guarantee each entering freshman no increase in tuition over the next eight semesters. Any increase in tuition would only apply to the freshmen entering at that time, and that too would be frozen for eight semesters.

"I believe we can do this if we commit ourselves to five principles: no growth, no specialized administrators, no varsity athletics, no staff and no long-term borrowing.

Robert was astounded. The proposal was revolutionary. But wasn't the college the place where such revolutions should begin?

Henry continued, "No growth means no new buildings, a great economy when you consider that electricians and plumbers earn twice what college instructors earn.

"No administration and no staff. By eliminating the bureaucracy, the salaries of the bureaucrats, and those of their secretarial and clerical support, would be eliminated. The administrators would be the professors. The clerical, secretarial and service people would be the students. This is even more practical today than it was twenty-five years ago, since word processing has made it possible for anyone to learn to type in three or four weeks and to turn out neat copy by correcting errors before they are put down on paper. Record keeping is similarly simplified by the computer."

"What about the dirty work?" Bob asked.

"When I was a kid, the school children eagerly volunteered to sweep the floors every day."

"Incredible." Bob said, "Today janitors are often better paid than teachers."

"Our janitorial staff would consist of students, volunteers, however reluctant. This would have the additional advantage of motivating them to encourage tidiness, since they would have to clean up the messes they and other students make."

"And you could follow the same policy for the student security guards. Upperclassmen could train freshmen in the routines of their duties," Robert said.

Henry injected, "Hardship jobs could be rotated where the seniority system is impractical."

"And discipline?"

"Severe misconduct, and dereliction of duty would be severely punished, including expulsion. We won't graduate people who refuse to learn how to behave. Teachers would be encouraged to participate in the necessary manual and clerical labor as an example to the younger people.

"Highly skilled work, such as electrical and plumbing

maintenance, would be contracted to outside firms. Only teachers would be paid a salary. Students would pay part of their tuition by their work. If necessary, the rest of their expenses could be met by student loans. Or scholarships, when we get them."

"But what about accreditation?"

The idea had bothered Henry. Perhaps those who opposed this new order of things would block accreditation and retard the growth of the college. But perhaps not. They may be so completely convinced that the new approach was impractical that they'd simply stand aside and wait for it to fall on its face. Chuck, of course, could help.

"The faculty?"

"No doubt we could recruit full professors from qualified retired people. And energetic young instructors from the ranks of graduate students in near-by universities, preferably doctoral candidates. The pay scale must be equal to that of the average small college."

"But the income would be higher, because they would be paid for teaching three semesters a year instead of two. And not at the reduced summer school pay scale, either. Or, if they preferred, they could take time off without pay. Pay them enough money and you can keep them from holding outside jobs. Good fringe benefits, too."

Robert dropped the papers to the desk, removed his glasses and wiped his eyes with his knuckles. This was beginning to be mind boggling. Fortunately, all of the burden would not be on Henry's shoulder.

SIX

In 1989, the town of Eunice, New Jersey had 8,452 residents. In outward appearance it closely resembled those communities which shared its borders — Madison, Chatham and Florham Park. Since it is approximately twenty-five miles from Manhattan, depending on whether you take the Lincoln or Holland Tunnel, an hour's drive with a little luck, it is regarded as part of the New York metropolitan area. The advantages offered by this location was responsible for a tenfold increase in property values over the past thirty years. The family which bought a house in 1955 for $25,000 could sell that house for $250,000 in 1985. Hence, the average family of modest means lived in a very valuable piece of real estate. Needless to say, many people found ways to profit from this development, particularly the realtor-politicians.

In a booming real estate market, land values can be manipulated by rezoning. Hence, it pays handsomely for real estate interests to engage successfully in politics, and for politicians to speculate in real estate. The prospects are even greater when, for one reason or another, one political party is dominant, secure that an election will not throw it out of power. Voters, on the other hand, are hesitant to change the status quo for fear that any change would be to their disadvantage.

In Eunice the political establishment of twenty or so men and women had been in political power unchallenged for as long as anyone could remember. They had done a good job administering the public affairs while enriching themselves. Years ago they had kept the town middle-middle class by excluding apartment buildings and by requiring every vacant lot in the town to be at least a third of an acre to qualify for a building permit. Combined, these policies kept Them out, since They could neither afford to rent nor buy. And that was the way most of the town's people wanted it.

Henry pulled the heavy loose-leaf binder from his bookshelf and opened it on his little desk, turning the pages until he found yesterday's notations. Immediately under it he wrote:

10-11-89 8:35 sunny, mild

In the nude, he weighed himself and recorded his weight as 154. Taking out his digital blood pressure machine, he secured the cuff around his arm, pumped it up and recorded the reading in his journal:

145/95

Not bad, he said to himself, but it could be better. He'd

continue taking his zestoretic. Lanoxin and quinidine gave him
no inconvenience except he no longer dared take an alcoholic
drink at bedtime. If he needed something to help him sleep,
he could always fall back on dalmane, but he tried to avoid it.
He was much too dependent on pharmaceuticals as it was, but
that probably went with growing old.

His journal was not only used to record important — to
him, important — happenings of the day. He also used it to
hold receipts and whatever other important papers he had to
keep. These he stapled to the pages, so he could remove the
paper without tearing it if he needed to. At one time he had
kept an elaborate alphabetically arranged file, but laziness had
often caused him to postpone his filing until the papers were
lost. He still used his file, but if he failed to file something,
he could always find it in his journal if he could remember
the approximate date he had stapled it to the page.

Today he made an additional entry.

*Decided to establish a no-frills college in collaboration
with Charles O'Malley. Have an appointment with
Brother Benedict this morning.*

Dennis Velez arrived promptly for his appointment. Henry
and Max conducted him to the sun-lit study where the aroma
of a pot of Creole coffee already dominated the room. Ignoring Henry's invitation to a seat on the sofa, Dennis appropriat-
ed Henry's easy chair, opening an expensive-looking attaché
case on his lap.

"Your invitation indicated a serious interest in Mr. O'Malley's proposal, Dr. Boudreaux, so I took it from there."

Henry had resolved that he would not be rushed into committing himself. "Before we go any further, Mr. Velez, explain this to me. How am I going to stretch two and a half million dollars to the extent necessary to pull this off? The property you expect me to acquire is worth at least several times the amount of money I have, and I disapprove of deficit spending in a situation such as this one."

Dennis continued to dig into his attaché case. "That's not a problem, Dr. Boudreaux. The real estate will cost you just two million dollars. That will leave you half a million in operating capital until you reach your break-even point. The borrowing you'll have to do beyond that amount should be insignificant. You should be debt free in a year or so."

Too good to be true, thought Henry. Which was another way of saying "suspicious."

"But why won't the brothers sell it to Mr. O'Malley or some other developer for a much higher sum?"

"Because the zoning code has this area zoned for educational institutions. And for one reason or another, no existing educational institution wants it, even at a bargain price. Maybe in a year or two, this situation will change, but the brothers need money badly, and they need it now. So you get a chance to pick it up at a bargain, provided you continue to use the land and buildings for educational purposes."

"But isn't that unfair to the Christian Brothers of England?"

"Perhaps, but there's nothing you can do to change the situation."

Henry was trying to think of reasons for dropping the whole idea. "But what if the half-million I'm reserving as working capital is not enough?"

"No problem. Mr. O'Malley is willing to establish a line of credit of a million dollars for you with the campus as collateral."

Henry thought again. He'd go over the whole matter thoroughly with Ray and Robert and Saul, his accountant, but if the data Dennis provided were accurate, he probably would never have to draw against that line of credit. And if he did, he could quickly pay it back out of tuition revenues according to the way he planned it.

As Henry pulled into St. George's faculty parking lot behind the administration building it occurred to him that he had never seen it so empty. Only one other car was in sight. Obviously, the lawns had not been mowed in weeks, probably not since graduation day. The grass was almost knee-high. Several months ago St. George's had graduated the class of '89 and closed its doors forever. Fortunately for Professor Henry Boudreaux, he had already retired by that time.

At the front door of the administration building, Henry turned the knob in vain; the door was locked. Perhaps Brother Benedict had forgotten all about their appointment. Old people are like that. Perhaps not. Going around to a side door, he checked and found it unlocked. There he entered a corridor so dust-covered he left foot-prints behind him. The door to the office of the president was open. Brother Benedict, who seemed to have aged and fattened considerably since Henry saw him last, sat at the presidential desk scrutinizing the papers which lay upon it.

"Come in, Henry," he said without looking up.

As he entered the office, Henry noted that it was as clean

as it was bare. The bookcases were all empty, the familiar "Oriental" rug was gone from the floor and the familiar pious pictures missing from the wall. But the room was immaculately clean, a testimony to Brother Benedict's fastidiousness. He had no doubt cleaned the office himself, ignoring the dirt in the rest of the building as irrelevant.

Henry sat himself down on the only other chair that remained in the room. What do you say in a situation like this? Certainly not "Glad to see you here presiding over the demise of the dream of your lifetime." The death of a college is a sad thing indeed.

Putting aside his paperwork, the monk apologized for his delay.

"You know how it is at our age. We have to hang on to our thoughts or we lose them."

He extended his hand.

"I'm sorry, Brother," Henry said taking his hand.

"I am, too, Henry, but I suppose it couldn't be helped. A school operated like this one was bound to fail. Too many conflicting objectives. I tried to convince the brothers that this was the case, but I just couldn't get through to them. Once the Vietnam war was over, we could not compete with the tax-supported county colleges without going co-ed, and Brother Sophos would have none of that. He feared that young women on the campus would convince too many of our novices that being a husband was better than being as monk. I said better now than later after we had invested heavily in their post-graduate education. I was overruled, and here we are now, out of business."

He shook his head and sighed. Henry was silent, waiting

for him to come to the point.

"Well, Henry, Charles O'Malley tells me that you are considering the resurrection of old St. George's and calling it Santa Sophia. I like the name, although 'holy wisdom' is tautology. All wisdom is holy. I presume it will be a Catholic school."

Henry shook his head.

"I hate to disappoint you, Brother, but wisdom does not necessarily have to be Catholic to be holy. What we have in mind is a nonsectarian college based on a Judeo-Christian foundation."

The brother was visibly disappointed.

"Well, half a loaf is better than none," he finally said. "I suppose you will want to have a look at the campus. We have added only one building since you left us. A dormitory for lay students. Brother Sophos wanted to attract students from outside the area. A mistake. A tragic mistake.

"You may not believe this, but some of those good Catholic boys demanded the right to bring their whores up to their rooms. Can you imagine such a thing? Can you believe that they were indignant when we expelled some of them for exercising this 'right'? We are here to educate Christians and Jews. Pagans we can do without. Now which building would you like to see first? The monastery, the novitiate, the classroom buildings, or that cursed dormitory?"

Henry made a mental note: Santa Sophia will have no dormitory.

"The students' dormitory," he replied. "I suppose the classrooms are much the same as I remember them."

As they strolled slowly over to the dormitory, Brother Benedict lamented the decline in vocations to the brotherhood and the advance of materialism which he held responsible for it. Walking through the dusty building Henry wondered what he would do with it. He would like to keep the community dining room. The students would require a hot meal at noon and there were not enough public eating places nearby to provide that service for so many new people. Perhaps coffee and sweet rolls in the early morning, and the faculty might find that they sometimes preferred community dining. Particularly those with no spouses.

The students' dorm had been designed differently from the novitiate. It had larger rooms, each containing two double-deck beds. Henry thought he could see the reasoning behind the design. The novitiate, with it tiny individual cells, was designed to discourage homosexual temptations, while the dormitory where each room accommodated four young men was meant to discourage fornication and the solitary sin. Lead us not into temptation.

On his way out, Brother Benedict again asked him if he would like to inspect the classrooms.

"Not today, Brother," he replied. "I'm assuming that they're much the same as when I taught there."

"Your assumption is correct," the monk replied, "except that air conditioning was added two years ago so that we could run summer sessions in competition with Seton Hall. Also there has been considerable deterioration. Brother Sophos was not interested in preventative maintenance."

As they moved slowly in the direction of the administration building and the monk's office, Henry's eye surveyed in silence the forty-five acre expanse of the weed-covered campus.

"What I can't understand," he finally said, "is why O'Malley or some other developer did not buy this campus and put up expensive new houses here."

"That's what we were hoping for," Brother Benedict replied. "Our order could certainly use the money. We're only twenty-three miles from Manhattan. At two hundred and fifty thousands an acre the land alone would have brought us more than ten million dollars. We have so few brothers these days that two-thirds of our classes are taught by laymen like you. The cost was backbreaking. Most Catholic families cannot afford our tuition and we don't have the heart to turn them away."

"A mistake the Jesuits would not make."

The monk ignored the rebuke.

"Unfortunately, the Zoning Board in this town stands in the way of development. These forty-five acres are zoned for an educational institution and the board, for reasons best known to itself, will not grant us a variance. Our creditors are on our heels, and we are forced to sell the school for two million dollars, a fifth of what it is worth. A pity! Of course, only an idiot would be willing to start a new college in competition with the tax supported colleges in the area. Oh, I'm sorry, Henry; I did not mean to call you an idiot."

Henry's reply was conciliatory. "Forget it. You may be right about my idiocy. But I'm ashamed to take advantageous of your misfortune."

"Don't be. If you don't buy St. George's, we'll be in even worse shape."

The next day as Henry was unlocking the front door of his house he heard the phone ringing. He was afraid he would not reach it in time, but he did.

"Dr. Boudreaux?"

"Yes," Henry replied.

"I have a suggestion that will discourage smoking in public. Now I know that you realize how unfair it is when a thoughtless smoker compels someone else to inhale his second-hand smoke. Yet how can a person retaliate without risking violence? I have a plan that is especially applicable to old people. You could use that million dollars to send out a piece of direct mail encouraging every victim of this ugly practice to fart. Bad air for bad air. What's sauce for the goose is sauce for the gander."

Henry couldn't believe what he was hearing. Then he laughed at the thought of sending out a million pieces of direct mail encouraging its readers to fill the air with bathroom smells and sounds whenever they were victimized by inconsiderate smokers. Then he realized that he may be hurting the feelings of the caller and apologized.

"And you name, sir."

"Kevin Burke, sir. And I also think we should put pressure on those congressmen who use our tax money to subsidize those people who produce tobacco, but that's another story."

"Well, Mr. Burke, regardless of the merits of your suggestion, I'm afraid we have already decided to use our money to open a college. Sorry. Good day, sir."

SEVEN

Henry Boudreaux and his friends, Raymon Donato, Gerald Walton and Robert Chang, were enjoying the fried chicken at Roy Rogers on Route 10. The price of the chicken was right, especially when you had coupons, and coffee was free to senior citizens. Besides, Henry was writing it off as a business expense, since they were there to discuss the future of their project."

"How do you like my suggestion?" Ray asked as he poured honey over the crispy deep fried chicken.

"It's very good," Henry replied without too much enthusiasm.

"But somebody else came up with something better? Right?"

"Yes and no. But I did receive what I consider a more practical suggestion, if only because it is in an area where we are experienced. It came from Charles O'Malley."

"*The* Charles O'Malley!" Ray exclaimed."

"Actually, it came from something O'Malley heard me say many years ago, only he revised my ideas and came up with what I feel is a practical plan."

When Ray had been briefed, with Bob's help, his excitement rose. "A no-frills college! My own suggestion is puny in comparison. Of course my idea of helping small businessmen survive and prosper is still valid, but I'd be the first to admit that many of them would refuse our help. Now tell me more about this famous alumnus."

"Well, Chuck — Charles O'Malley — wants me to establish a new college on the campus of bankrupt St. George's College. He wants me to get it going with the help of a few of my old friends. His idea is the use of the economy of smallness for increased efficiency, something I had advocated many years ago when I pointed out to my students that the economics of size is a two-way street. As a firm gets bigger it tends to become more efficient in some ways, but only at the expense of becoming less efficient in other ways.

"Finally, it reaches a point where the efficiencies of its increased size are more than offset by the inefficiencies. Each kind of business has its ideal size in terms of efficiency and cost per unit of production. Beyond that point its unit cost of output increases with its increase in size."

"People might ask, 'Why would an administrator want to go beyond that point?' " said Walton.

"Because administrators have goals of their own, goals often in direct conflict with those of the stockholders. For example, they may want to leave their imprint on the firm. They may be trying to improve their résumés so they can bargain for promotions, or salary increases, or to improve their chances of getting better jobs with other firms. The list is long, if not endless."

"I think I see what you mean," said Robert Chang. "Applied to education, it means that the per-student cost of a large institution would tend to be greater than that of a somewhat smaller institution. To say nothing about the quality of education."

"Not to mention the cost of expansion, a policy so dear to the hearts of administrators."

Raymon smiled. "I like it."

"Enough to come out of retirement and help me turn this college into a viable institution?"

"Enough. I'll give you four years."

"Good enough. That means you would see the first freshman class graduate."

"Do you think I have four years left in me?"

"A tough old Dago like you? You have at least five. And what about you, Gerald?"

For a long while Gerald did not reply. Finally he said, "Count me out, Henry. Charlotte and I have been making plans to move to Nevada for months now. We're tired of this climate. We're tired of this congestion, of living in the most densely populated part of the most densely populated state in the nation and all that goes with overcrowding. Waiting in line everywhere we go. Always being in somebody's way and always having somebody in our way. And the rudeness that goes with it as some people try to beat the rap. Like the young man I saw push an old lady aside to steal her taxi."

Henry was visibly disappointed. Finally, he said, "But look at the positive side. It also means we have the best stores and the best hospitals in the world."

Gerald had thought about that. "Yes, but computer shopping nullifies the advantage of large stores, and as for hospitals, we would not need so many hospital beds if we were not confronted with so many things that harm our health. No, Henry, we've already put our house up for sale."

The same day the announcement of the opening of St. Sophia's College hit the newspapers, André Wilson appeared. He did not phone; he simply turned up at Henry's front door where Max greeted him with a bark that was not a threat but an announcement. Max got mixed reviews as a guard dog. His huge size and his deep growl were enough to intimidate any intruder but he slept so soundly that even an inept burglar could probably steal the television set without awakening him. And he was almost always asleep.

Henry was neither surprised nor pleased by the arrival of his visitor, a former colleague. He knew that André would have a difficult time getting a new job after St. George's had closed. His demands were too great and what he had to offer was too little. A fat Black man of great charm, in Henry's opinion he had little else to offer an institution of higher learning. While their relationship had been cordial — he had been a guest in the Boudreaux home several times — Henry did not want him on the faculty of Santa Sophia. Particularly, as a full professor, since this would mean, automatically, a seat on the Board of Trustees.

They were seated in the living room, the only spacious

room in the house. André was at his charming best, slowly sipping his scotch-on-the-rocks.

"I'd really appreciate it if you'd take me on, Henry. Now I know we haven't always been the best of friends, but I know you're too big a man to let that stand in my way."

A master of the understatement, Henry thought; in his last year at St. George's he had been barely polite to the man. He was no hypocrite. He could not be a close friend of a man he could not respect. "Actually, André, we have no vacancy on our staff for a man with your unique talents. Sorry."

"But I've been unemployed since last May, and I have no contract for next September. All my applications have been politely turned down."

"Have you applied — outside the New York Metropolitan area?"

André frowned. "What you really mean is have I applied at any of the Negro colleges down south. Well, the answer is 'no.' I like New Jersey and I have no intention of leaving."

"So do I," Henry replied, selecting his words very carefully. "I understand your position, André. Sorry I can't help you."

His uninvited guest then resorted to the technique of the implied threat. "Perhaps you'll soon be a lot sorrier."

He left in a huff.

That evening when Henry told Grace about the incident, she said, "That's too bad. I like André. Are you sure you can't find a place for him?"

Henry's reply was grim. "I'm sure. You see, Grace, André is a very likable person but a very poor teacher. His classes were popular with many of his students because he required

very little of them. In the way of work, that is. What he did
require was that they agree wholeheartedly with his opinions.
There was even some doubt that he corrected their papers.
Some said he gave out A's to those who agreed with him in
class and B's to the rest."

Grace snapped on the television set. To a commercial.
"Did he ever do any work toward his doctorate?"

"He worked very hard. But the man just doesn't have it.
You see, he's a memorizer. As I see it, he probably made a lot
of A's in graduate school because he memorized his professors'
lectures and a few of their favorite authors, and gave back to
them exactly what they gave him. When it came to writing a
thesis, that was another matter. You can't fake creativity. So,
actually, he never even got his Master's, but because he got
such good grades in his courses he was allowed to begin work
on his doctorate. Eventually, this policy became bankrupt.
He had to produce an acceptable Master's thesis and to be able
to defend it. He couldn't."

Grace wanted to know why such an incompetent· teacher
had not been fired.

Henry replied, "Perhaps it was an oversight that could not
be corrected later without considerable embarrassment to the
administrators."

Henry had moved into the office vacated by Brother Benedict. Dennis Velez had suggested that he do so, "to get the
feel of the place." Dennis was Charles O'Malley's liaison man.
A large brawny man, Dennis looked more like his Irish mother
than his Puerto Rican father. He was soft spoken and conciliatory, but his very size was intimidating. He assured Henry

that, although there were many time-consuming legal formalities to go through before Santa Sophia became a legal entity and took title to the campus, the outcome was never in doubt. Henry believed him because he had no reason not to.

This morning he had an appointment with Dr. Patricia Principe. It bothered him somewhat, because she had applied for the very position he had just denied André Wilson. He hoped Wilson would never learn of this meeting. He believed in keeping the number of his enemies at a minimum. Dark-skinned and dumpy, Patricia did not look old enough to be retired. The shallow crow feet around her eyes seemed only to a enhance her handsome face.

"Dr. Boudreaux? I believe I met you years ago at a meeting at Pace University."

"I remember," he lied politely.

Patricia had assumed that since he was an economist he knew something about her work, but she was taking no chances. Along with her résumé, she had included a photocopy of her biography as it was listed in *Who's Who in America*. From it he learned that she too had a Ph.D. from Fordham, and that she had been active in the American Economic Association.

Patricia was so enthusiastic about Santa Sophia — the whole concept — she offered to teach without pay if that's what it took to get on the faculty. She didn't need the money. Her late husband had left her well off and she had neither children nor grandchildren to consider.

"I appreciate your generous offer," Henry was saying, "but I cannot accept it. You see, Dr. Principe, Santa Sophia must stand on its own feet. It must pay its own way. If it cannot do that, then the whole idea lacks validity."

He paused a moment, then continued.   "We cannot base our
financial policy on the exploitation of our faculty as too many
colleges have done in the past.   If we cannot pay our teachers
an appropriate salary, then we shouldn't be in business.   If the
Board of Trustees approves of your application, as I am sure it
will, you will be paid twenty thousand dollars a semester —
sixty thousand dollars a year — just as any other full professor."

"Well, this is a refreshing surprise," she said.   "Usually,
administrators try to pay as little as they can get away with
paying.   And while it is not necessarily true that you get what
you pay for, it is generally true that you don't get what you
don't pay for.   Now tell me more about your plans."

He told her about Joseph White and his generosity, about
Charles O'Malley and his helpfulness, and before they knew it,
half an hour had passed.   Henry was pleased to discover that
his first impressions about her were reinforced.   She would
make a valuable addition to any faculty.   Walking her back to
her car, he was exuberant, talking so rapidly about his plans
she had little chance to get a word in edgewise.

Unlike André Wilson, Rudolph Schaefer did phone. Henry
was surprised.   He had thought that with the kind of résumé
that Schaefer had, getting another job in the New York City
area would be a snap.   Apparently, this had not been the case.
Anyway, Rudy notified him of his availability in a manner
that suggested that he really didn't care very much whether he
were hired or not.   Henry knew him only by reputation, since
he had joined St. George's faculty after Henry's retirement.

Rudy was just the opposite of André.   Brilliant, creative he had completed most of the work on his Ph.D. by the time he was twenty-three. Yet he, too, was a poor teacher. He expected his students to be as brilliant as he was, which of course was not the case. As Henry saw it, if a teacher has contempt for most of his students, he is teaching in the wrong school.

Rudy also felt that because his salary was low he was justified in neglecting his teaching. Those things which interested him got his meticulous attention, but teaching was not one of them. It was the kind of job he expected to do with one hand tied behind his back. Henry knew this; the academic grapevine is quite effective. When he told Rudy that there was no place for him on the new faculty, his reaction was one of apparent indifference. That relieved Henry's mind. He would have had a hard time trying to explain to Charles O'Malley why he did not hire this brilliant young man who already had the reputation of a world class scholar.

EIGHT

It is not often you can have a cook-out this late in the year, but when you are given the gift of such a beautiful day, it would be a shame if you didn't take advantage of it. The sun was shining brightly, the breeze was mild. It was almost noon and Henry was preparing to broil hamburgers for himself and his guest. Dennis had suggested the Afton but Henry wanted something a bit more private, such as his own back yard. In deference to the notorious Jersey mosquitoes, a circular screen house sat on his patio. There they could eat without being eaten.

The raw hamburger patties waited in the chill of the refrigerator. They cost as much as steak and were worth every penny. Henry never had any luck broiling steak, so he never tried; that was Junior's job when he was around. Henry did a good job on hamburgers if he did nothing else but watch them. As usual, he was having trouble getting the charcoal started. Perhaps it was time to try one of those propane gas grills like the one Junior was always urging him to get. Some day, maybe. Now let's see. He had lettuce and scallions from his garden, and tomatoes from the supermarket. His home grown tomatoes, picked green in September before the first frost and ripened indoors, were all gone. On the table beside the cordless telephone sat a bottle of vintage French burgundy, uncorked, breathing.

Max notified him that his guest was approaching.

"Come in, Dennis," he said, first checking his hand for grease, then extending it in greeting.

"It's good to see you, Dr. Boudreaux."

Dennis was too well-mannered to call an old man by his first name, not even when asked to do so.

"We'll sit in the screenhouse even though the mosquitoes are gone. A month ago they were fierce around here," Henry said.

"Fierce everywhere," said Dennis as he accepted the invitation without hesitation. The charcoal was now glowing, so Henry excused himself and went to get the meat and salad dressings from the refrigerator.

"How is your college coming along," his guest asked as Henry placed four large raw hamburgers over the glowing coals.

"Well, we have four other professors signed up, good people. I know three of them personally. We have accepted seventy-five students for the fall semester, expecting fifty."

"Why so many no-shows?" Dennis asked. "Didn't they all have to put down a deposit?"

"They did. But for some of these Santa Sophia is their second, third or fourth choice. If the college which is their first choice accepts them in the meantime, they will simply default their deposit."

"And what if they don't? What if all of them show up in September."

"We're prepared to accept them, although we'd rather not."

He turned the hamburgers over with a spatula, carefully because they broke so easily. Juices fell to the glowing charcoal and sizzled, sending out a mouth-watering aroma. Honey bees buzzed around, frustrated in their futile attempts to penetrate the screen. It reminded him of when he was a soldier in England — that must have been forty years ago, no, more than that. It was August of 1944 — forty-five years would be more like it — when trying to wash your messkit meant to risk being stung by aggressive British bees.

By the time the buns were toasted, the burgers were done. Dennis liked his medium-rare, which gave the short-order cook some degree of latitude. Well-done means risking drying out and burning.

"Excellent," Dennis commented, biting down. "Couldn't be better. By the way, are you having any difficulties I could help you with."

"Only one. I have not been able to hire enough junior faculty members. We can get along without them, but the quality of our instruction would suffer. These are the people who would head the seminars, the discussion groups essential to our approach to college teaching."

"Have you tried offering higher salaries?"

"Not in the budget. We'd have to increase the tuition too much. Besides, we have a contract with September's freshmen that their tuition would not be increased during the next eight semesters."

"What about fringe benefits?"

"We already have the usual. Blue Cross-Blue Shield, Major Medical, Accidental Death."

Dennis looked up. "You know, Dr. Boudreaux, I've paid as much as ten dollars for a hamburger at the Elephant and Castle in Manhattan but never for anything this good."

"You can thank Don's for that; he makes the patties. I just grill them. As I was saying, what other benefits could I offer?"

"What about housing?"

"The novitiate had small cells for the novice monks. No, too austere. The new tenants would get claustrophobia. Now the students' dorm has large rooms, each made to accommodate four students. We could offer them to our instructors rent free. How's that for a fringe benefit?"

Dennis stopped chewing and held his napkin in front of his mouth. "At least it's a start. Let's have a look at that dormitory."

They did, the following Monday.

David was spending Saturday morning with his grandfather. They played several games of open field bocci, one of the few games an old man can play with a little boy. David was not allowed to win; in Henry's mind that would be setting a bad precedent.

Then David said, "Pipère, let's look for four-leaf clovers.

That was even less strenuous than bocci.

"Not over there, David," he said as the boy began to search the grass of the bocci area. "Let's look at the corner of the house."

"You mean there's none over here?" the child asked.

"Well, there may be. But I've found that if you look in a place where you've already found one this summer, you're more likely to find more of them near by. And there's none early in the season, before the lawn mower and the rabbits get at the clover."

A few moments later, David cried out, "I found one. Oh, no!"

He had pulled up two three-leaf clovers that seemed to be one four-leaf clover.

Finally, David saw another that looked promising. He was more careful this time, counting the four leaves several times before he announced his triumph.

"Remember this, David. It's easier to find something if you know when and where to look."

"Not bad. Not bad at all." Dennis surveyed the room. Naked mattresses covered the two double-deck beds. Two double dressers faced each other across the room. They examined one of the four closets and found it ample.

"That ought to do it," Dennis said. "Why don't you notify the deans of all the graduate schools within an hour's drive from here that your instructors will get one-room apartments rent free."

Henry agreed, adding "Since most graduate schools offer their courses in the late afternoon or evening, the instructors could do their teaching here in the morning and early afternoon and still have plenty of time to get to class."

He knew that he was correct, still he felt that he might be missing something. Finally, he had it. He wanted as his instructors doctoral students, not simply those working on their master's degree. And most of the doctoral candidates were married. He pointed this out to Dennis.

"So we'll convert some of these rooms into three-room apartments," Dennis said, nonchalantly. "That would be an even bigger attraction."

"Big enough to justify an hour's commuting time," Henry agreed enthusiastically. "That way we could get instructors studying at Princeton, at Fordham in the Bronx and Rutgers in New Brunswick and Seton Hall University in South Orange."

Then his enthusiasm sagged when he realized that this would cost a lot of money.

"I'll look into this, including what it would cost. Our bank would loan you the money to make the improvements, of course," Dennis said.

Henry hesitated. "But that would violate our policy of not going into debt."

Dennis had expected this. "Maybe. Maybe not. Your idea of going into debt, as I recall, was assuming an obligation that you could not pay off in a year."

"Yes."

"Maybe — just maybe — we can do it. I'll contact a contractor who specializes in this sort of thing."

A week later, coincidentally while Henry was broiling a hamburger for himself, with Max lying patiently near by awaiting his taste, he answered his cordless phone. It was Dennis.

"Well, Dr. Boudreaux, I had a contractor over at that dorm. He gave me a ballpark estimate of ten thousand dollars each to convert dormitory space into three-room apartments if you get at least ten apartments done."

Henry hesitated and calculated. That would push his break-even point back at least another semester. Could he live with that. It seemed as if he'd have to.

"Tell him to type up the contract, Dennis," he said, hoping he was not making a mistake. Then he got out that special address book listing the deans of all the graduate schools in the greater New York area.

NINE

That November had cool days and, unpredictably, even a few hot days. What was predictable was its cool nights. Dennis Velez phoned Henry to say that Mr. O'Malley had arranged for a story about the new Santa Sophia College in a national magazine. He advised him to prepare to answer his correspondence promptly.

"Promptly! I haven't even answered the mail I got two months ago."

"Probably you shouldn't bother with that," Dennis said. "You'll only run into a lot of requests that you couldn't comply with in view of the commitment you have already made to Santa Sophia. Your job, if you don't mind me saying so, is to get this thing going and that will take all the energy you and your colleagues have and then some."

Henry realized that this was true. This myth that an old man is as fit to run a complex business as a young man was just that — a myth. He and his colleagues would have to conserve their energy and expend it wisely.

Already the campus was beginning to look like a campus. A contract landscape gardener had cut the tall grass and weeds and hauled it away. He wanted to plant shrubs and flowers but the Board of Trustees voted "Not this year." Following their own philosophy, and over the protests of Jimmy Lucia that they were not janitors, the instructors had cleaned and scrubbed the administration building, including the second floor which had served as living quarters for the professed brothers. Leaky roofs had been sealed, noisy plumbing silenced and windows caulked. Heating bills in this climate are expensive enough without waste.

The first floor of the building would be retained as the administrative offices of the college, just as it always had been. To the right of the president's office was the board room. Today the large table where former college presidents had once met with their advisors now served another purpose. Lunch was being served on paper plates from half a dozen cartons supplied by the Four Seasons Chinese restaurant.

Two recently hired instructors were introduced to the Board.

"Bill Caffery from St. Louis University, historian. Working for his Ph.D. at N.Y.U."

He nodded.

"Barry Prisco. Math major. Working on his Ph.D. dissertation at Fordham."

Barry nodded, wondering why the senior faculty had not been introduced. Apart from Doctor Boudreaux, he knew none of them.

Henry addressed the newcomers. "Since you were hired

very recently, you probably want to know where we stand at present.

"We have a vast amount of mail to answer since we received nationwide publicity. Apparently, we have struck a chord. I hope it is more than our offer of lower tuition, but I'm not sure. We shall soon get some idea, however, since we are all going to be working on that mail.

"It has been agreed that all the correspondence will be divided among the full professors, each of us responsible for the reply."

Prisco looked at Caffery, then asked. "And what are our duties in this matter?"

"Secretarial. You'll sit at a word processor and prepare the replies."

Obviously, that answer did not sit too well.

"Sorry, Dr. Boudreaux, but I can't type. I don't even know the keyboard of a typewriter, much less than how to use a word processor."

"Within two week you won't be able to say that, Mr. Prisco. Doctor Mott will teach you."

Prisco wondered about what kind of crazy situation he had gotten himself into. So did Caffery.

Max barked loudly and fiercely, a bark that would make the boldest intruder tremble with fear. Henry thought that it must be a United Parcels person with a package for Grace. Max hated United Parcels personnel with a vengeance. There was no UP person.

Instead, Ernie stood in the doorway. "I read about it in the paper, Mr. Boudreaux. How could you? How could you throw away all that money on education when there are lives to be saved?"

"Because I had a decision to make, Ernie. There's just so much any one person can do, and I felt I didn't know enough about problems of health to go in that direction. Now in the field of education I — "

"Education, hell. My grandson is dying and all you can think about is educating a bunch of snobs. What good is an education. I'll bet I made more money — and spent it too — than half of your educated idiots."

"Maybe if you had saved some of it, instead of squandering it like a drunken sailor you could solve the financial problems you now face," Henry replied icily.

For a moment Ernie stood there with his mouth open. Finally he said with a bitterness Henry had not witnessed in years, "Squandered, is it? You think a working man ain't entitled to nothing. Well, I'll tell you, I'm entitled to every bit as much as you. And I'll tell you something else. If that kid dies, I'll hold you responsible."

With that he turned his back and walked away. Pity and revulsion fought each other for Henry's soul. Neither won, although the struggle continued for a long time. Henry's conscience was clean, in terms of what he had actually done. It was in the area of what he could have done, should have done and yet did not do where his conscience bothered him. Would Ernie's attitude turn out to be one more such situation? Henry was very much upset by Ernie and his antics. He felt a guilt that he knew he shouldn't feel. Why should he, of all people, be held accountable for someone else's misfortune? Had anyone — and that included Ernie — offered to share *his*

misfortunes? Of course not. That's not the way things work.
Only a mind warped with guilt, like Ernie's, could think that
way. But the bad feeling which his attitude had engendered
was still hard to shake off.

Then something happened that made him forget completely
Ernie and his problem. Max's friend, the letter carrier, had
rung his doorbell, and Max was barking his head off. There
was a certified letter he had to sign for. Since the return
address on the envelope was that of a law firm he never hear
of, he tore it open nervously.

The message was short. When Henry read it he became so
sick he though he would vomit. He sank to his chair, and
allowed himself time to recover. Then he read it again, this
time one word a time. There was no mistake. His son Patrick
had employed an attorney to have Joseph White's second will
contested in favor of the one previously made, naming Henry
Boudreaux, his wife, and their sons as his heirs. The lawyer
maintained that he could prove in court that Joseph White was
mentally incompetent when he made the second will. His
client, however, was amenable to an out-of-court settlement in
the interest of family harmony.

Pat! The little punk! His own son! Henry had done everything he could for him during his stormy childhood and his
prolonged adolescence, and now he pulls this thing. Damn his
hide. Damn those goddamned lawyers and their contingency
fees. Well he won't get away with it, not if I have to spend
the entire legacy fighting him. But how?

Chuck O'Malley, of course. He'd know what to do. He
took out his address book and looked up the telephone number
of Dennis Velez.

TEN

In New Jersey December is entitled to be ugly, and it usually is. But the tinsel of the holiday season camouflages much of that ugliness. Grace and Henry always enjoyed Christmas, especially when the entire family gathered together to celebrate as it usually did. Christmas of 1989 would be somewhat different; the family would gather at Henry Junior's home in Florham Park. Last year Junior and his family had flown in from California. Since then, they had moved to New Jersey.

Traditionally, the Christmas Season begins the day after Thanksgiving Day, although in recent years merchants have jumped the gun with their merchandising. Decorations, carols played and replayed with monotonous repetition, crowded stores, crowded streets. For weeks, Inez and Junior had planned every detail. The tree could not be artificial, of course. Junior made a meticulous search in a dozen different locations before he found one that satisfied him, and by the time he had it in its stand he had become dissatisfied. He turned it around, a few degrees at a time until it was at least acceptable, then secured it in place with two thin, almost invisible guy wires.

Decorations were applied by the two children. David, who was now four years old, insisted that he could hang ornaments on the lower branches. Inez allowed him to do so, knowing that later she would have to rearrange the decor. Hélène was five years older than David and could not be so easily fooled. Her decorations had to remain were they were. This year the colors were silver and blue, with plenty of angel's hair. However, neither the mouth-watering aroma of roasting turkey nor the lilting voices of happy children could erase the under-lying gloom felt by the adults.

Not entirely. Patrick would not be with them this year. "I tried to talk him out of it," his brother said, "but it didn't work. Off hand, I'd say that it's a case of pride. Pride and a bad conscience. Having tried unsuccessfully to break Uncle Joseph's second will in the face of your opposition, he just can't face us. I blame that lawyer. I'm sure he convinced Pat that you would settle out of court to avoid a scandal."

"Pat should know me better than that," his father said. "And he knew Joseph wasn't out of his mind. Everything Joseph ever did was carefully thought out in advance. Other-wise, how could he have beaten the stock market, which he did until the day he died? Even his suicide was well thought out. Unlike some of those despondent people who jump out of a window and kill an innocent person below, he made cer-tain that no one else would be hurt when he destroyed himself.

I was confident that any judge in this district would see it that way, so I told his lawyer to go chase some other ambulance. Fortunately for us, he did."

Happy Hélène was busy stacking boxes wrapped in shiny colored paper under the tree. The lights blinked merrily, reflected in shiny silver and blue balls. "It's still a bad thing to have your son at odds with you," Henry continued. "And Pat is probably not that happy about it either. This is the first Christmas he has not been with us, with the exception of his year in Paris."

Grace wanted to change the subject. "Well, I'm glad you told that attorney off. It was attempted extortion, pure and simple. Just like Ernie Hause."

Too late she realized that she had brought up a subject that should not have been mentioned on the happy occasion. Her husband compressed his lips into silence. Fortunately, the phone rang. Henry, Junior, answered it.

"Can you pick me up at the station in Madison?" said the voice on the line. "The cab drivers seem to be taking the day off."

"Pat!" exclaimed his brother. "Can't say that I blame them. I surely will pick you up. See you in about ten minutes."

So it was a merry Christmas after all. During dinner no one mentioned the estrangement between Pat and his father. Inez had roasted the turkey to perfection, until its moist meat nearly fell off the bone. Yellow turnips for Pat and Grace; white turnips for Henry Junior and herself. That girl thinks of everyone, her father-in-law said to himself; I wonder if Junior realizes how lucky he is. No doubt he was attracted to her by her beauty, but in this case beauty was a lot more than skin deep.

She served a good California white zinfindel with dinner. The stuffin' had been made by Henry, omitting the chestnuts from part of it because of doctor's orders. Desert would have to wait. They were already uncomfortably full. When they retired to a living room lit by the blinking Christmas tree, Pat said, "Dad, I owe you an apology. I know now that I was wrong. I guess I knew it all along. But you must admit that your ethics are unusual."

"I don't know about that," his father said; "I only know that a man must do what he must do."

"Kant's categorical imperative," Junior commented.

Pat put a cigarette into his mouth and was about to light it when he remembered that Inez hated smoke in her house. He put the cigarette away without lighting it.

Henry sipped his cognac from a brandy sniffer. "You know, boys, I've always said that to get ahead financially a person needed a year's pay as an investment. Then, if he never touched either the principle or its earnings, he could not only stay out of debt but, with a little bit of luck, retire in style."

His sons wondered why he should bring this up again. They had heard it before.

"Well, I once had an opportunity to "earn" five thousand dollars — a year's pay at the time — simply by raising the grade of a wealthy student from an F to an A. When I politely refused, his father told me that he could easily get the change made for five thousand dollars by going to a certain Brother, but that he would prefer that I get the money. He knew about my illness; he knew I could use it. I was so angry that a religious person would sell grades that I tutored the young man free of charge, and gave him a re-examination. He earned an honest A. I have never regretted it. Today the young man is a highly successful businessman, not so young any more, and we're good friends."

His sons were silent for a long time, until little David asked, "When are we going to open the presents?"

Pat gazed at the huge stack of presents piled under the tree, embarrassed that he had not contributed to it, embarrassed that when the family sat in a circle around the living room there would be none for him. Hélène did the sorting, proud of her ability to read names. Pat's chagrin vanished when she handed him his first present, addressed in his mother's handwriting. Good old Mom; he didn't deserve her.

The pile in front of each member of the family continued to grow until everyone, including Pat, had eight or ten boxes, wrapped in shiny paper and tied with colorful ribbons in front of him. Then mistress-of-ceremonies Hélène announced, "Now, Pipère, will open a present?"

Henry's arthritic fingers struggled with shiny ribbons, then a shiny box which he opened to reveal the expected pair of new moccasins amidst ooohs and ahaas from everyone. They knew he loved moccasins.

Now, moving clockwise, it was Grace's turn to open one of hers. The ceremony continued until chaotic piles of gifts covered the floor and the adults had to help the children pack the mountains of discarded wrapping paper and ribbons into plastic garbage bags, pitying the garbage men who would have to collect an extra-ordinarily heavy load on their next round.

January is usually a hateful month and January of 1990 was no exception. Snow made driving hazardous, and so many motorists just didn't seem to realize just how hazardous, thought Henry as his Omni picked its way through the icy streets toward Santa Sophia's campus. Confident in their ability to handle any driving situation, they didn't seem to realize that there are a lot of old fools like him whose poor vision and slow reaction should be reckoned with. The parking lot near the administration building had not been plowed of snow and he wondered if his car would become snowed in before he left. That would mean walking home, which he did not relish in this kind of weather, even though it was only five blocks away.

No other cars were parked in the parking lot, which did not surprise him. Of course, Patricia Principe and the two instructors who would probably be in their offices. He hoped so. If the work piled up any higher, he'd have to call in Manpower, Inc. again, and he hated the extra expense temporary workers meant.

"Henry," Patricia called after him as he passed her door. "I need your advice."

She handed him a set of papers.

"What do you think of him?"

Henry quickly scanned the three pages. The boy had a poor transcript. Mostly C's and D's, but heavily sprinkled with A's. No B's. His SAT scores were even more unusual. In verbal, 715, and in math 725. Very high.

"What we have here, Pat, is a brilliant but lazy or undisciplined student. He studied those subjects he enjoyed, and ignored the rest. I'd venture to say he never brought a textbook home. Let's accept him. If we can't stimulate him to learn in a systematic way, no college can."

"That's exactly the way I feel," Patricia said.

Barry Prisco was at his computer, a disorganized pile of papers on the desk. For several minutes Henry stood there observing him. The computer hummed softly, as he clicked away at its keys. He had mastered the keyboard quickly, learning his A-S-D-F-G's in a month, and now he was keyboarding at 45 words per minute.

"Very good, Barry."

"Thank you, Doctor," the young man replied.

"I'm happy to see you become so proficient so quickly," Henry added. "Now you will suspend work on your present project."

"But I've almost caught up."

"It can wait. I want you to do what you came here to do. I want you to teach word processing to two new instructors who will be joining us today."

Prisco looked pleased. He had not only acquired a valuable new skill; he had been paid to acquire it. He could not keep from asking, "What about Bill Caffery?"

Henry did not even look up from the paper he was reading. "He was fired. For goofing off. He was warned three times, and every time we warned him, he gave us a lot of guff. I hope we have better luck with the next two."

Prisco suddenly felt very vulnerable. Then he realized that he need not be. He did his work well. He fitted in. Caffery got what he deserved.

The crocuses were in bloom, shrugging off the chilly northern breeze which persisted into April. The sun shone so
brightly that young people were tempted to underdress; usually
old people were not so foolhardy. The administration building
had been heated to a comfortable seventy-two degrees. No
point in risking pneumonia.

Ray was addressing the assembled faculty; "Personally, I
like the idea, but I wonder how it will sit with the accrediting
agencies. And what about offering Spanish as the only foreign
language?"

Henry defended his policy. "Our resources permit the
offering of only one foreign language. Which shall it be?
Personally, I'm partial to French. After all, my name is
Boudreaux. But the vast majority of non-English speaking
people in the Western hemisphere speak Spanish. That's reason
enough."

"Do we have anyone on the faculty who can teach Spanish?"
"We do. I."

"Yes, I know," said Ray, "but most of them did not major
in the language they propose to teach. I'm afraid the accrediting agencies will not find that acceptable."

Henry intervened. "We are not here to submit to the arbitrary rules of bureaucracies which are more concerned with
defending their turf than they are with quality instruction. A
good teacher is not necessarily one who knows his field thoroughly, but one who is successful in passing on to his students
that which he does know. In other words, we don't need a
Spanish major to teach first year Spanish. That is an artificial
requirement, made with the interests of teachers in mind
rather than that of the students."

"I agree."

"I also agree," Ray said. "But you must admit that we're asking for trouble if we row against the current."

Henry smiled. "Isn't that what Santa Sophia is all about?"

ELEVEN

The slender young man extended his pale, elongated hand. "Dr. Boudreaux, I am Alfred Koenig."

Henry shook his hand. "Mr. Koenig."

"Don't you have any air-conditioning in this place?" Alfred asked, sweat running down his reddened face.

"Yes, we do," Henry replied. "It is now broken, but summer is almost over, so I think we can do without it until next year. It will be more economical to have it repaired in the fall."

He was thinking about the revenue from the tuition of the coming semester that he needed to pay for this expensive repair job. He was also thinking of all the hot summers he had taught summer school without air conditioning. No point in mentioning that.

"Seems masochistic," the young man replied.

"Or heroic."

Henry told him a story of Alexander the Great. His entire army was crossing a desert and dying of thirst. A soldier found a little water in a rock and brought some to his general in a helmet. Alexander gazed at the water, his mouth watering, looked up at the drooling soldiers around him, and dumped the water on the ground. A cheer went up from the parched throats of his troops. Morale revitalized, the soldiers marched out of the desert.

"Sounds crazy to me; but I'm no Alexander," Alfred said. "I'm only — "

The phone rang. Henry apologetically excused himself to answer it, feeling that it was somewhat unfair to the boy in his office, but without a secretary to screen his calls it was inevitable. He made a mental note to train several of the incoming students as secretaries.

"I'm sorry, Miss Appleton," the boy heard him say, "but the committee did not recommend your admission. I told you so by mail immediately after the decision was made."

Silence. More silence.

"I'm sorry, but that's our decision. Good luck in your applications elsewhere." Before she could get another word in, he had hung up.

"The girl just didn't meet our requirements," he said by way of explanation to Alfred. "Now what can we do for you?"

"I got the brochure you mailed out. What I want to know, sir, is electives. Your brochure mentioned nothing about electives. I'd like to major in communications arts."

Henry had been through this before. You offer a program, and they contact you to inquire about a program you don't offer.

He kept his temper.

"Then I'd recommend Seton Hall University. I hear that they have a good program in communications arts."

"I looked into it, sir, but the cost of their tuition is twice as much as yours."

Henry smiled. He had heard that one before.

"The reason why our tuition is lower is because the fewer the number of courses offered, the more economical it is for the institution. By offering no electives, we cut costs to the bone."

"Oh."

"What we offer, sir, is a liberal education in three years at affordable tuition. This will give the student a chance to undertake his professional training on a graduate level, which is where we believe professional training should be given. But only after the student has received a liberal education." Koenig nodded in apparent agreement.

"Now to come back to our foreign language requirements, the Board of Trustees debated this matter at length. It was finally agreed that few students who do not major in a foreign language learn enough of that language in college to work within it. And most of what they do learn is soon forgotten. Therefore, we wanted a language program designed to provide a thorough grounding in one foreign language, a foundation upon which to build should the student desire to study the same or another foreign language at some time in the future. In addition, it should improve his or her knowledge of English."

"A few other questions, Dr. Boudreaux. What is your tuition?"

"At present, eighteen hundred dollars per semester."

"And fees?"

"There are none. We believe that fees are but tuition increases in disguise."

"And what about scholarships?"

"In each section the student with the highest quality point average for the semester will receive a full scholarship for the following semester. As the scholarship fund increases, we hope to award two, three or more full scholarships each semester."

"What about your parents income?"

"Irrelevant. We don't take it into consideration. Otherwise, we might find ourselves awarding scholarships on the basis of the most convincing lies."

"But is that fair to low-income students?"

"At Santa Sophia we are more concerned with promoting scholarship with our scholarships than we are with the redistribution of income."

After a long pause Koenig said, "Can I call you back on this?"

Henry answered immediately, "Let's see. You have already been accepted for the September freshman class. If I don't hear from you by the day after tomorrow, I shall assume you will have made other plans and give your seat to the next applicant in' line. Of course, you would still be free to apply for admission to our January, 1991, class."

Opening his mail, Henry read,

Dear Dr. Boudrow:

You'd think he'd take care to spell my name correctly, Henry said to himself.

Your mandatory requirement of four years of Spanish does not meet my requirements. I have had two years of Spanish and I would like to take another foreign language. Please let me know why that is not possible.

   Cordially,

   Edwin Kosikoski

Henry started to make a note on the margin of the letter for Prisco to answer it, changed his mind, and turned to his computer. He typed

Dear Mr. Kosikoski:

Then he hit Control and the number five key. The computer hummed as the monitor read

It would seem that Santa Sophia does not offer a program that meets your requirements. However, I am certain that in the Northern New Jersey area you will find an institution that does.

   The best of luck.

   Henry Boudreaux, Ph.D., President

He then printed two copies of the letter and placed them in Prisco's in-basket for mailing.

It was a hot day early in August and Henry usually had enough sense to stay out of the sun on hot days. Only today he had a job to do which just wouldn't wait. In early spring little David had planted carrot seeds in the garden. Unfortunately, the few plants that did come up soon died. Now David was asking about his carrots, so Henry had gone to the supermarket and bought carrots with their tops still on. These he was planting in the same row in which Dave had planted his barren seeds. Tomorrow they could harvest the carrots. The kid would be delighted with the fraud.

Henry thought that it was unusual to be interviewing such an applicant for a professorship. The new semester was only a week away. The applicant was over seventy, he would think, although in theory it was illegal to ask his age. As if the date of his graduation from college did not provide a good indication.

"Dr. Thompson, your résumé is quite good. Unfortunately, we cannot offer you a contract for next semester. There is a vacancy in European history for the semester after next in the rank of associate professor."

The man looked more indignant than disappointed.

"But I retired as a full professor," he protested.

"I can see that," Henry replied, "but full professorships are limited in number and we already have a full complement."

"I never heard of such a thing. I . . . ".

"I don't think you have. You see, Dr. Thompson, at Santa

Sophia — unlike at most other colleges — the full professors run the college. They constitute the Board of Trustees. This is why our charter limits their number. A committee that is too large is unwieldy. I am sure you must have heard the one about a camel being a horse designed by a committee."

Dr. Thompson forced a reluctant laugh.

"Now, associate professors are paid the same salary as professors and they teach twelve hours a week. That is because they have no administrative duties and they are under no pressure to publish."

"I never taught more than six," was the reply.

"Here you would teach twelve."

After a long pause Dr. Thompson said, "Could I start next semester?"

"Sorry. Our vacancy is in the following semester. A two-semester contract at twenty thousand dollars a semester."

The applicant had a desperate look on his face. "But I need that job now."

Henry knew he had to be firm. "But we don't need *you* now. We hire on the basis of our needs, not yours. That's only fair to the students who pay tuition."

Dr. Thompson did not reply. He simply got up and slowly walked out of the room.

TWELVE

When Santa Sophia opened its doors to its first freshman class in September of 1990, two days after Labor Day, the heat of a lingering summer presented a problem. Although the classrooms and offices, the library and the cafeteria were air conditioned, the system had broken down and it had not yet been repaired. The first few days were even more hectic than Henry had expected because the students and some of the faculty were unfamiliar with their surroundings and it was a situation of the blind trying to lead the blind.

On the other hand, the curriculum could not have been more simplified; all students were classified as Freshmen I and only six courses were being offered: mathematics, sociology, economics, English, Spanish and geography. Every student's program was identical to that of every other student. Every student attended a lecture given by a full professor. The two instructors, low men on the totem pole who assisted the professors in teaching the subject, were always in the audience. One of these operated the video camera.

No questions or other interruptions of the lecture were permitted. Those with questions were asked to jot them down and bring them up during the seminar sessions which followed two days later. These were conducted in part by professors and in part by instructors. Video tapes of the lectures were available in the library for review, or for students who had missed a lecture. Audio tapes of the lectures could be bought or checked out of the library and taken home. The semester got off to a good start.

The first faculty meeting was a luncheon meeting, held two weeks later. In spite of their announced policy of eating lunch with their students, the only policy consistent with their philosophy of constant education, the professors and instructors brought their trays of food into the board room. Everyone was excited. They were about to add a chapter to the history of higher education, or so they thought.

Professor Donato could hardly control his enthusiasm. "Well, Saul, how do we stand?" he asked.

Professor Saul Schwartz was a C.P.A. with a Ph.D. in Economics. He was also a mathematician of extraordinary ability. For years he had taught accounting at Rutgers-Newark while maintaining a lucrative accounting practice in that city. Now, retired from Rutgers and returning to college teaching, he had turned his practice over to his unmarried daughter, Alicia, so that he could devote full time to Santa Sophia where he would double as bursar and Professor of Mathematics. He would also teach student assistants the rudiments of electronic bookkeeping. He was anxious to put into practice a computerized system of accounting which he had devised, a simplified system which the average college student could learn to operate within a few weeks. Inclined to be dramatic, he enjoyed a pregnant pause before answering his colleague.

"We are right on target, Ray. Right on target. We matriculated fifty-six students this morning, and the average SAT was 1,003. This means that our target of an average SAT score of 1,000 has been met."

He paused, dramatically. "This score is significant, since, among the private colleges of New Jersey it is exceeded only by those of Princeton, where the average in recent years has exceeded 1300, and Drew where it has exceeded 1100. Of course, we're not in the same leagues as those two, but it is comforting to know that we lead our own league, followed by Seton Hall, Fairleigh Dickinson and St. Peter's where the average SAT is in the 900s, to say nothing about those colleges where the score is in the 800s or even lower.

"So we're starting out with good material," Raymon said. "Now all we have to do is make the best of it."

"Amen," Saul said.

Ray Donato still had his misgivings about putting too much emphasis on SATs. "Taking examinations is a skill in itself," he argued. "Not all intelligent students have that skill. I would prefer to place more emphasis on their transcripts. The records of what they did during their four years of high school."

"But we have gone over all this before, Ray," Henry protested. "The consensus was to give equal weight to grades and SATs, then to factor in extracurricular activities. As long as we don't rely too heavily on any one criterion, I believe we'll be all right. By the way, this green pepper steak is excellent. I'll have to tell Robert so."

Patricia nodded. "Which is exactly what you would expect of Bob Chang. I was wondering why he wasn't with us today."

Henry replied, "Now you know. He's teaching the undergraduates how to cook, a skill which, I maintain, is an important part of any liberal education. I'm afraid that until Bob has trained competent cooks, he'll spend all his time in the kitchen. I don't have him scheduled for classes until next semester. He says that he doesn't mind because skill in cooking is more important than skill in philosophy."

"Spoken like a true philosopher," Saul said. "But, say, Henry. You're a good cook. How did it happen that you end up as president of this college and Bob Chang as an instructor in the art of cooking?"

Henry grinned. "We flipped a coin for it and I lost."

The five professors sat at one end of the huge table and the twelve instructors at the other end. Below the salt, as it were. Plenty of room, Henry thought, but if things go the way we hope they will, we'll soon have to have our faculty meetings in one of the classrooms."

"I think I'm going to like the technique of a weekly lecture by a professor followed by two meetings of the class in the form of discussion groups," Patricia said. "Of course, we know that the larger universities have employed this method for many years with varying degrees of success."

"With this exception, Patricia," Henry said. "Our discussion groups will be limited to eleven students; those at the universities are usually at least twice that size. I feel that with the smaller group the shrinking violets will have no opportunity to shrink. Furthermore, our full professors will have personal contact and interact with all their students. They won't just lecture to them without ever knowing their names."

Vinnie Mott agreed. "But it *is* expensive. We have to pay salaries of twice as many instructors this way."

"Yes," Saul said, "and I'm sure it's worth every penny. Time will tell, of course."

The others seemed to be concentrating on their pepper steak and fried rice. Henry hated to spoil their lunch, but he felt he had to. "There's one thing that bothers me."

They gave him their attention while continuing to eat.

"Last summer I made an expenditure which I had not originally planned to make. I converted the students' dorm into an apartment house, a fringe benefit to attract married instructors. I don't have to tell any of you about the housing shortage in the New York metropolitan area since World War II, and the high rentals where there is no rent control. For a graduate student from outside the area, the lack of housing can cause him or her to avoid a university in the area. Well, the idea to provide rent-free housing for our instructors was a good one. We got more qualified applicants than we could use."

"Then what's your complaint?" Patricia asked.

"We had to go into debt. The cost over-ride for remodeling the dorm was double the initial estimate. In other words, it cost us twice as much as I had expected."

"Can we live with that?" Vinnie asked between chews.

"Yes. But what if there are other hidden costs we could not anticipate? They could destroy us."

"Let's not be pessimistic," Saul said.

Two weeks later, Robert Chang dropped by Henry's office.

"Well, Henry, how are your classes?"

"It feels strange to be teaching Spanish," Henry replied; "I haven't taught Spanish in fifty years. I had to start off by teaching myself the Spanish which I had almost forgotten."

"You know, Henry, I really am looking forward to teaching Logic next semester. I feel that I'm doing a lot of good by teaching cooking, but since I have begun to review my Logic, hardly a day goes by when I don't become aware of somebody trying to peddle a commodity or a service or an idea by perverting logic. By the way, how are the others doing?"

"What you'd expect. Chaos. These first four weeks have been a nightmare which you were fortunate to miss, but by last Friday we had begun to hit our stride so I know the situation is not hopeless. It will still take us the rest of the semester to get into the groove."

"And next semester? Will you continue through with Spanish II or will you teach Spanish I to incoming freshmen?"

"Both," Henry replied.

"My students are quickly mastering the art of cooking, so I think I can go back to teaching Philosophy next semester, although I'll still be on hand as a consultant in the culinary arts."

Robert inquired about the health of Grace, their sons, their daughter-in-law and their grandchildren. Henry reciprocated.

The student security-guards seemed to be doing their jobs in spite of the usual boy-girl distractions. The only question was who was going to guard the guards. It was not that any serious crime was likely, but rather one of attention to duty, and, indirectly, to Santa Sophia's liability for anything that went wrong during their inattention. In such a situation, it was quite possible for a guard to hide away somewhere when he should be patrolling the campus. Annoyed by the lack of a sense of responsibility on the part of some supposedly adults, Henry had lectured to them several times on the subject. Still he occasionally found a guard studying on the job, or asleep or even making out. Finally, exasperated, he transferred a repeat offender to the janitorial staff. The others were shocked into paying closer attention to their jobs.

The janitorial service had less problems, although some students made no secret about their displeasure at being required to sweep and scrub floors. Their griping ended when Henry volunteered for janitorial service. At first they were shocked. The president of their college sweeping floors and emptying waste paper baskets? Then they got the message. If he could do it, they surely could. And besides, when the next freshman class came on the campus in January, they would no longer be low men on the totem pole and move up to less onerous duties.

One afternoon, while Henry was pushing a broom, he told them a story.

"During the Great Depression I was happy to get a job in a factory. I didn't ask 'What kind of job is it?' I was so happy to get it. The foreman looked me over and said, 'Take that broom and sweep that floor.'

" 'But I'm a college graduate,' " I protested.

"The foreman replied, 'In that case, I'll show you how.'"

THIRTEEN

"How's it going, Bob?"

Robert Chang, Professor of Philosophy, Vice-President of Santa Sophia College, and formerly Professor of Culinary Arts, had met Sean O'Connell, American Lit and dean of studies, on the snowy, windswept campus. January's snowbanks were piled high, pushed there by students manning snow-plows. Freezing winds were blowing much of it into their faces, particularly their eyes. Hurriedly, they moved toward the nearest shelter, leaning against the bone-chilling wind.

Sean caught his breath as Robert replied. "Great. I introduced the Square of Opposition this morning. This afternoon every student is smugly convinced that he knows almost everything there is to know about logical fallacies. How's the semester going?"

"January registration went well," the dean replied. "Much better than September registrations. More than a hundred students, fifty-three Freshmen I and fifty-eight Freshmen II.

I guess we're old hands at it by now. We have seven students who qualified for Freshman Spanish by examination, so we are giving them each six credits toward graduation and allowing them to take Sophomore Spanish III instead."

Robert had classes in O'Malley Hall, originally so named by the good Brothers in honor of their patron and tactfully allowed to remain so by their successors. He remained with his friend only long enough to thaw out his frozen ears and face. Sean returned to his office for his appointment with John Atkinson, Freshman II.

"You're Mr. John Atkinson?" he asked the sole occupant of his outer-office.

"Yes," the young man replied.

Sean wondered why he didn't say "Yes, sir."

"Come on in and sit down, Mr. Atkinson. What can I do for you?"

Atkinson was baby-faced, short and fat. His pale moon-shaped face was overburdened with a thousand freckles. "Well, Dr. O'Connell, I need your permission to drop calculus."

"And why do you want to drop calculus?"

"I'm just not mathematically inclined, I guess. I just can't seem to get that stuff."

Sean leaned back in his chair.

"Did you discuss this with Dr. Schwartz?"

"No. I only got a C from him in algebra last semester. I could hardly expect him to see my point."

"And what about Mr. Barrow?"

"He's worse than Dr. Schwartz. He thinks that anyone who is dumb in math is an idiot."

Sean walked over to the window and stared out at the

blowing snow. Drifts seemed to be building up quickly.

"Did you know, Mr. Atkinson, that Charlemagne only learned to read in his old age, but he never learned to write? Do you know why?"

"No, sir," the boy replied, apparently to both questions.

"Perhaps he didn't try hard enough. Perhaps his great achievements had left him an exhausted senior citizen."

Silence.

"Let's give it another try, Mr. Atkinson. I'll arrange to have Miss Salazar tutor you without charge for the rest of the semester. After that you're on your own."

"Miss Salazar? That would be great, Dr. O'Conner. Don't worry. I won't let you down."

Sean smiled. "With the prettiest instructor on the campus as your tutor, Mr. Atkinson, I'm sure you won't."

The next meeting of the Gang of Seven, as a few of the instructors were beginning to call them, took place on a dreary day. But most winter days are dreary, aren't they? Most professors hate most meetings most of the time, and bad weather does not improve their disposition. Henry had a hard time calling the meeting to order. Sean O'Connor took out a cigarette, and was about to light it when he was stared down by several others. He put the cigarette away without lighting it. His first angry impulse was to walk out of the room. Who needs these intolerant people? He surely didn't. But he did need the college, so, like King Henry IV who thought that the city of Paris was worth a Mass, he thought that Santa Sophia was worth a cigarette.

"Gentlemen," Henry said before he realized that this ignored the presence of a lady. Patricia smiled her forgiveness.

"Folks," he said, folks for want of a better word. "We have reached another crossroad. During this semester we must hire more associate professors and instructors if we are to be fair to our students. What's your opinion on the subject?"

The debate that followed lasted forty minutes, to the annoyance of all participants. Finally, it was agreed to promote one instructor, Prisco. He would graduate from Fordham in June with a Ph.D. Henry was not too enthusiastic about the decision. He feared it would open up a Pandora's box when the other instructors learned about it.

"That still leaves us needing four more instructors and two more assistant professors or associate professors."

Saul had an idea. "I think they should be Associate Professors. Otherwise, — " The debate was resumed and lasted another tiresome ten minutes before a weary consensus was reached on the subject.

Henry turned his swivel chair slightly to face the microphone on his desk. Simultaneously, he pressed the "play" button and the "record" button and dictated into the microphone:

"Letter number sixty-eight, for my signature. Dear Mr. Anderson: Thank you for your letter of February 3, 1990 and your kind words about our 'noble experiment in education.' Your offer to donate a new building to Santa Sophia to be named in honor of your mother is most generous. Unfortunately, we cannot accept it. To do so would compel us, morally speaking, to put it to good use, and, in view of our philosophy of 'no growth', we cannot do so.

"May we suggest instead that you set up the Margaret Anderson Scholarship Fund so that qualified students could get into college without getting into debt?

Gratefully yours,"

Noticing the amber light of his inter-com winking, he pushed another button. "Yes, Burton?"

"A gentleman to see you, Dr. Boudreaux. Dr. Simmons."

They shook hands. "Matt! It's so good to see you."

The brown hand that Henry shook was long and slender, like a pianist's. Matthew Simmons was tall and thin, ascetic looking. His head, Kojak-bald, was probably shaved since his gray mustache was thick and well trimmed. Impressed by his résumé and Henry's recommendation, the Board of Trustees had already voted to offer him a professorship, so this interview was simply a formality for the record. He would be the first African American on the senior faculty.

The interview lasted for half an hour. The two men had many acquaintances in common, and most of this time was spent comparing reminiscences. Finally it was Matthew who brought it to an end, saying that he had another appointment.

Henry replied, "If it is for a job, when you get there, tell them you already have one at Santa Sophia as dean of students. Our Dr. O'Connor is leaving."

Matthew smiled as he accepted Henry's extended hand. "I'll do better than that," he said. "If I may use your phone, I'll just call up from here with my apology."

As Santa Sophia's newest recruit to the faculty left, Henry hoped that all such interviews were as easy. The one that immediately followed was anything but easy.

The first impression he received of Stewart Mueller was that he was too young to have retired from anything, except perhaps professional football. A big man, all muscles, he must have looked out of place in a lecture hall. Yet his handshake was hardly bone crushing. A considerate man. Pale blue eyes blinked in a tanned face. His expensive brown suit bore signs of wear. Henry could not help but glance down at his shoes, highly polished, worn at the heels. This man needed a job, and Henry wanted to give him one. But not at the expense of his students.

Melted snow had frozen, turning the streets into ice-skating rinks. Sanding trucks had worked through the night to improve traction, but not always successfully. Henry wore rubber overshoes, hoping he would not slip and break any of his old bones. Half sliding, half walking he finally reached his office intact. There a stranger waited for him.

"Dr. Boudreaux, I'm John Gregario, an attorney. I represent Professors André Wilson and Rudolph Schaefer."

Henry was puzzled. "We have no one on our faculty by those names."

"Perhaps you have," the lawyer replied politely, pointedly waiting for Henry to absorb the significance of his words. "You see, Dr. Boudreaux, it is our contention that Santa Sophia College is really St. George's College operating under a new name. We therefore contend that you are legally bound to honor the contracts St. George's had with its faculty, including Professors Wilson and Schaefer."

Extortion, Henry thought. Legal extortion. He knew of cases in industry where judges had ruled in favor of employees of factories and offices which had been taken over by other corporations. Would a judge do so in the case of a college? You could never tell. A jury trial? The college would probably fare even worse from a jury trial. Juries tend to favor individuals over institutions.

The attorney saw the look of shock on his adversary's face and concluded that he had a good chance of settling out of court. He handed Henry his card. "There's no hurry. My clients are willing to settle for two years' salary to avoid the scandal of going to court."

When the lawyer left, Henry felt so dizzy he had to sit down.

"Bastards," he murmured. "Extortion. That's all it is." They know that there's no merit to their case. They know Santa Sophia only acquired the buildings and grounds of a defunct institution. What if it had been converted into a factory? Would they have sued for jobs in the factory?

Yes, they would, he concluded. If they thought that they could get money out of it. And you never knew, these days.

The possibility of treacherous snowstorms hangs over early April, but April's snows are the most beautiful in urban areas. They melt before they have a chance to become dirty. Three days later, spring pulled a surprise. The weather was beautiful. The sun shone brilliantly, although not enough to fool the forsythia into opening their yellow petals, nor warm enough to induce the three elderly professors to walk coatless across the campus to their cars. But the young people all over the place wore less than they should. Like the coed who overtook and passed them. Coatless and hatless, she wore skin-tight admire-my-ass jeans which could not be ignored. They were old but not blind.

"Ever think of getting married again, Paul?"

Paul did not answer.

"Now if you could have someone like her for a wife? Smart, young, sexy, full of vitality?"

Paul knew that this was not a question but he treated it as one.

"Only if I could first bathe in the fountain of youth. As I see it, the only young woman who would consider me for a husband now would either be a gold-digger or some nut with a father complex. Neither would make me happy very long."

He was severely tempted to tell them that he and Patricia Principe were to be married the following week.

If Henry had sought any reassurance from his friend, Julius Adams, he did not get it.

"Back up a bit, Henry. You've lost me. When I went to college so many years ago, I knew only two kinds of teachers. Those who had their doctorates, whom we addressed as 'Doctor' and those who didn't. We addressed them as 'Mister' or 'Mrs.' or 'Miss'. What's all this stuff about 'instructor' and 'associate professor? *et cetera?*" And why is it so important, especially when there's no money involved?"

Julius, a retired engineer, had dropped by the office of the president to check on his friend.

"I sometimes forget about those things when I am talking to people who are unfamiliar with the campus hierarchy. Sorry about that."

He paused.

"You see, Julius, on the campus we have a hierarchy, just as they have in the army and in the church. The lowest rank of the faculty is Instructor. Usually, this is the rank of the beginner. Usually, but not always, it commands the lowest salary. Instructors hope to be promoted to the next rank, that of assistant professor. Usually — but not always — the assistant professor is a Ph.D."

Julius obviously needed further enlightenment.

Henry continued. "If the Board of Trustees recognized unusual talent in a candidate, he could be promoted to the rank of assistant professor before getting his doctorate. The rank carries a higher salary and more responsibilities."

"Usually?"

"Usually."

"And the associate professor is a notch above the assistant professor. Right?"

"Right. Many do not rise above this rank, even teaching in colleges and universities all their lives."

"Which is why those who do are kind of stuck-up about it."

"Absolutely. At any given time about fifteen percent of a faculty consists of full professors. Usually."

FOURTEEN

Part of the problem was that the recruitment of associate professors was, as expected, a major roadblock. Younger men and women were scared away by the experimental nature of Santa Sophia, and older people had difficulty changing their thinking to adjust to the new roles they would have to assume. It wasn't a question of salaries. There Santa Sophia was competitive. It was a case of a teacher having to fit into the over-all pattern alien to him, a way which many thought violated academic freedom. On the other hand, a dean must be able to compel his faculty to stick to the syllabus, otherwise a coordinated program is impossible.

Henry's meditations on the problems of a college president were interrupted when Max picked up one of his shoes and, with a let-me-out-now moan, went to the back door. He continued to moan until Henry took the shoe away from him and let him out. The dog went to his corner of the back fence where he augmented the compost heap. He promptly returned and scratched at the back door, demanding immediate admission.

The second semester was almost over and Henry was getting desperate. None of the candidates who had applied for associate professorships had been acceptable. Either that or, after the interview, they had decided that they would prefer to teach elsewhere. Finally, a suitable candidate was found in the person of Dr. John McCabe. He would begin his work within a week. John was drawn to Santa Sophia by its unique goals and teaching methods. He expressed faith in its future, but he was also curious about the college that had preceded it and had since gone out of existence. Why? Would Santa Sophia face the same difficulties that drove St. George's out of business? Having taught at St. George's for many years, Henry was in a position to enlighten him.

At the turn of the century an English-born widower had lain dying in his eighty-room mansion. He has no direct descendants. His nieces and nephews who, up to this point had neglected him shamefully, hovered over his death-bed like vultures. "I'll fix 'em" he said to himself. "I'll leave most of my estate to charity."

He thought of the Christian Brothers of England, a Roman Catholic order of monks who operated a number of private high schools for Catholic boys. Although he was not a Catholic, he had attended such a school. But he had never gone on to college. It occurred to him that he could bequeath to that religious community his mansion to start a college for future members of the order. Better educated teachers would result in better educated high school students. As insurance against his kin contesting his will, he bequeathed each of them the sum of a hundred thousand dollars with the provision that they would not contest his will. The institution was named St. George's College, in honor of the patron saint of its benefactor.

Well, at first everything went well. The monks not only educated their own members, but those of other teaching religious orders as well. When the veterans of World War II flooded America's college campuses immediately after the war, the Brother Superior saw an opportunity to expand. St. George's would be open to all Catholic males and to those brave non-Catholics males willing to put up with the monks' heavily indoctrinated courses. Classroom space for evening classes was rented from near-by parochial schools and wherever other suitable space that could be found.

The next problem: Should they rely on members of their own order for faculty? Hardly. These brothers were needed in the classrooms of the high schools they operated throughout the country. So they hired laymen to teach at St. George's, even some laymen who were not Catholic. Henry Boudreaux was among the first.

The school prospered economically if not academically. With money earned from educating the laymen the Brothers expanded their activities by erecting a classroom building. Enrollment of laymen dropped in 1950, but when war came to Korea many young men discovered that they had a vocation to the brotherhood. Brothers were clergy as far as exemption from the draft was concerned.

A few years later when St. George had again begun to

flounder, the Vietnam war increased the number of young men going to college. Attendance at a college provided them with the means of deferring their draft status without becoming monks. Although a number of brothers had suddenly discovered that they really didn't have vocations after all, the increase in tuition-paying lay students filled their classrooms. St. George's was more prosperous than ever.

When America's armed forces withdrew from Southeast Asia, the academic balloon burst. Lay students became fewer every year. The number of professed brothers and novices also decreased at an alarming rate. Another crisis existed. Could St. George's College survive this one? One realistic possibility was to go co-ed and admit girl students to the campus. The brother superior recoiled from this suggestion in horror. Instead, he accepted the suggestion to build a dormitory and recruit students from outside the area.

That failed, too. The cost of the dormitory was a back-breaking nine hundred thousand dollars. Meeting the payments on the money borrowed was so difficult that the aging Brother Superior had a nervous break-down. Benevolent Brother Benedict was called in to liquidate St. George's.

The committee marched into Henry's office in single file and stood in a semi-circle around his desk. "Dr. Boudreaux, we want to protest the unfair increase in tuition."

"Ladies and gentlemen, that increase was necessitated by an unanticipated increase in costs."

The spokesman was nervous. "We know that, sir. What we consider unfair is that those who matriculated a semester ago are not subjected to the increase."

Henry twisted his stiff neck. That pain was back again. He regarded the young people with what patience he could muster.

"Because the students of Freshman II have a contract with Santa Sophia to pay $1,800 in tuition each semester until they graduate. The Full Professors, acting in the capacity of a Board of Trustees, thought that this arrangement makes it easier for students to plan the financing of their education."

He hesitated. "Of course, this also applies to you people of Freshman I. The tuition you had to pay for your first semester, namely $1,900, will be the same you pay every semester for the next seven semesters but future Freshman I classes will be subject to a change in rates. Do you see anything unfair about that?"

No reply.

"If you do, we'll have all the students vote on it. If they vote it down, of course, then all students will be subjected to the same increases whenever our costs go up, and the same decreases in the unlikely event that costs go down. What do you want? It's up to you."

"We'll talk it over, and let you know, Dr. Boudreaux."

As they left, Henry told himself he probably would never see this committee again. He never did.

This faculty meeting was confined to full professors. It was the first mild sunny day in April of 1991, and all those present would have preferred to be outdoors celebrating the arrival of spring, but the problem was such a serious one that no one was absent. Although the promised greenery was nowhere to be seen, the bright outdoors beckoned them as they sat at one end of the board table, involuntarily glancing out the window from time to time.

Henry described the crisis brought on by Wilson and Schaefer. Unnecessarily. It was all too familiar. Summarizing the situation, he said, "This is our problem. Is it better to pay these people eighty thousand dollars each to stay away from Santa Sophia, or to fight them as a matter of principle, knowing we may lose?"

Raymon Donato was the first to speak.

"I say no. Pay an extortionist and others with equally invalid claims will shake you down. There'd be no end to it. If we're going to be destroyed, I say we should go down fighting."

"Perhaps they're bluffing. Perhaps if we offered them ten thousand dollars they'd settle," Patricia Principe volunteered.

"Perhaps you're right," Saul said. "Even so, news of the settlement would appear in the papers and probably other former St. George's faculty personnel would put in their claims."

Ray Donato nodded his agreement. "Even if no one else did, if it got no further, we'd still end up with egg on our faces. I would rather go down fighting."

"What if Wilson turned this into a racial issue?" Patricia asked. Unthinking, everyone looked in Matt Simmons' direction, then nervously and self-consciousness looked away.

"There's no 'if' about it," said Matt, the only African American present. "Mediocre people always play that card to the hilt. This puts the opposition on the defensive. You have to prove you are *not* guilty of racial or ethnic or religious or sex discrimination. It's like trying to answer the rhetorical question: When did you stop beating your wife? I hate people who do that, and I certainly don't want one of them on this faculty. I vote that we tell them to go to hell."

His colleagues agreed.

Early in June when second semester grades were posted a girl student, Susan Smith, was extremely dissatisfied with her grade. She accused her instructor, Vito Vitelli, of having an affair with her. She said that he had threatened to flunk her if she didn't. The dean recalled her records from the computer, and concluded that she had deserved to flunk, that the C she had received had been due to the quizzes Vitalli had been responsible for. She was placed on probation and ordered to repeat the course. Henry summoned Mr. Vitelli to hear his side of the story.

Dr. Simmons, the dean, was also present. The instructor defended himself by saying that the relationship was entirely voluntary on her part.

"We only collaborated sexually, as is the right of all consenting adults. I made no promises."

Henry had great difficulty remaining calm. "Voluntarily? How can it really be voluntary when you have such power over her?"

Vito shrugged this off. "But you know as well as I do, Dr. Boudreaux, that I have no real power to give grades. I only give objective quizzes which are corrected by the computer. Dr. Principe gives the essay exams in this course and she corrects them herself. I only merge her grades with mine and record the results."

"But how did the girl see the situation?"

No reply other than a shrug of the shoulders.

Dean Simmons turned his back and said, "Mr. Vitelli, if you met three tough-looking guys in a New York subway train who ask you for a ten-dollar contribution, is it voluntary? They have the power of life and death — and you have no way of determining whether or not they will exercise this power. How would I define power?   The ability to resolve a conflict of interest in one's favor. If I can do that, I have power. That's exactly what these three young men have. You know it.   You are intimidated. If you are not intelligent enough to see that, then you are not sufficiently intelligent to be a college teacher. You're fired."

Vitalli sprang to his feet. "I can't believe my ears! You old fogies must still be living in the middle ages. This thing happens all the time. It's practically a fringe benefit in college teaching. High school, too."

"Hold it," Dean Simmons cried out. "Mr. Vitalli, I don't give a damn who you screw as long as it is not one of our students.   This is not a question of private morality, which is your own business, but of a conflict of interest, which is ours. This is a question of stupidity and irresponsibility and unethical conduct. If you can't see that, you're too stupid to qualify for a position on our faculty."

Vitality shouted back, "I wouldn't want to teach for you anyway. But you haven't heard the last of this. It's about time for the junior faculty to get some protection from arbitrary actions on the part of high-handed administrators, even if I am not here to see it."

The following day Susan played her trump card.   "Mr. Vitalli said that I would get an A for the course, and I maintain that even if he is no longer on the faculty, Santa Sophia has no right to change his grade."

"You realize, Susan that, Mr. Vitalli was only an instructor. When you were a freshman you were told that only professors could give grades."

The dean was measuring his words carefully. He had been expecting this.

"I don't remember," she replied.

"I'm sure that most of the students in the assembly hall will remember."

"Maybe I wasn't there."

"Maybe. But you were given a pamphlet which clearly stated that fact."

"I don't remember getting a pamphlet, and I certainly don't remember reading it."

Patricia hesitated. So this is the way it's going to be.

"Well, I'll have to look into the matter more closely, Susan," she said.

The first thing Patricia did was to look at Susan's high school transcript. Atypically, her grades were almost all A's and C's. This could mean that she was a brilliant student who neglected those subjects she disliked. Or that some of her teachers could have, for one reason or another, given her higher grades than she deserved. Then she looked at Susan's record at Santa Sophia. Five C's and a D. Strangely enough, the D was in Spanish, a subject in which she had received an A in her last year of high school. It was beginning to look like Susan Smith's grades depended more on her relationship with her teachers than on the quality of her work.

The problem was on the agenda at the next faculty meeting. "A ticklish situation," Ray said, and everybody agreed.

"Why not give her the damn B and be done with it?" someone said.

"It's not that simple," Matthew replied. "If I read the pattern correctly, the girl will not abandon her tactics and next semester will bring a repetition of last semester. If we don't stand our ground, she could screw her way all the way up to a Ph.D. I'm opposed to submitting to blackmail."

"She could hurt us badly."

"She will hurt us badly, no matter what we do."

"Then let's stand up for a principle: grades at this college can neither be bought nor extorted."

As expected, they soon heard from Susan's attorney. They gathered all the evidence they had and handed it over to the attorney Dennis Valez had recommended. The matter was quickly settled. Henry got a phone call from one of the junior partners of the law firm, Willard Gelenski, a former student of his.

"My boss has reached a tentative agreement with Susan Smith's attorney. She will have to be paid twelve thousand dollars for the year she 'wasted' at Santa Sophia, twenty-eight thousand dollars for tuition in a comparable college, and another ten thousand dollars for her legal fees. Oh, yes there's another two thousand dollars to a private investigator."

Henry wanted to scream. His attorney had sold him out for a quick fix. But why scream at Willard? He was only the bearer of bad news. This would throw back their break-even date at least a semester, maybe two. And he had not even thought of the sizable fee he would have to pay his attorney.

When he got that bill, he whistled and picked up his phone.

"Willard? Do you know how much your boss charged us for the Susan Smith case? You do? Well, it will take all the tuition collected in a semester to pay that bill alone. And that doesn't include the settlement."

Willard allowed him to ramble on until he was out of breath, then said, "No, Doc. I didn't realize that. But you must realize that we're a high-price firm, but we get results. And that costs us money, so we have to pass those costs on to you. No, I don't think it would do you any good to talk it over with a senior partner. Our fees are not negotiable. They have to be charged off as a cost of doing business. So my only suggestion to you, Doc, is that if you can't afford the costs of doing business, you should get out of business."

"Willard! Willard?"

He had hung up.

FIFTEEN

Santa Sophia's first summer semester was difficult on both teachers and students. The students had the idea fixed in their minds that they were going to "summer school." By this they meant scanty clothing and watered-down courses, usually given by junior teachers who needed money badly. These teachers could not earn that money if they flunked all the students who deserved to flunk. They had to compete with the "practical" teachers who offered substitutable courses. If a course did not attract enough students to pay its way, usually ten or twelve students, it was dropped and its teacher became unemployed.

So summer school was often something of a joke. The students paid their tuition. Their teachers earned that little extra money essential to their economic survival, and, by mutual understanding, nobody worked very hard. Therefore, it came as a shock to many of Santa Sophia's students when they received low mid-term grades. The turmoil was so serious that Henry had to call a special assembly to meet the problem head-on.

"You were told at the very beginning of the summer *semester* that this was not a summer session in the usually accepted sense of the word. Obviously, you didn't believe me; look at your mid-term grades! Now you do."

A murmur of protests buzzed around the auditorium. They had expected something more conciliatory. The speaker waited for quiet.

"Years ago, the summer program was diluted because it was recognized that the heat made it impossible for students and professors to do their best work in summer. Many colleges closed down in summer, which was their approach to the problem. Others permitted only a limited number of summer courses to be applied toward a degree, implicitly recognizing the inferiority of summer work.

"When air conditioning first came to the college campus, it was found exclusively in the office of the president."

Laughter.

"Then the obvious was finally admitted: With artificial climate control in the library and classrooms, students could do high quality work all summer long. In many places, however, even with air conditioning, summer school remained but a shadow of the spring and fall semesters. There were reasons for this, but most of them were not academically sound. Therefore, Santa Sophia rejected the whole idea of summer school and replaced it with a summer semester, with the same quality of work delivered by its teachers and the same quality of work demanded of its students as during the other two semesters. Only then can we, in good conscience, offer a bachelor's degree in less than three years.

"So my word to you, ladies and gentlemen, is that you must change your attitude. Your alternative to doing quality work in the summer semester is to drop out for the summer and delay your graduation by a semester. It's up to you."

The very next day the air conditioning unit broke down. Henry was compelled to pay the technicians triple-time in order to get the work done at night. Many students cut classes, relying on the video tapes for the lectures. Others sweated it out, literally, during the thirteen days required for the repairs. Henry was tempted to mention that he had taught summer school, literally sweating it out, many summers ago when air conditioning was found only in movie theaters, but prudently he refrained from doing so. Nobody wants to hear from old fogies like him about how tough things were in the good old days.

Hard-to-get parts for the air conditioning system had to be flown in from Ohio, then returned when they didn't fit, and other parts ordered in their place. Henry did sweat that summer, especially when he got the bill.

"Good morning, Dr. Boudreaux."
"Good morning, Miss — "
"Pryer. Dolores Pryer."
"Yes, of course. Please excuse my bad memory. Actually, I should remember the names of every student at Santa Sophia, since I have taught every student at Santa Sophia. But at my age it may take a while to come up with a name. Of course, I haven't taught you since two semesters ago. How are you

getting along?"

Obviously, the question was rhetorical, and so was her answer. Henry mopped his brow with an already damp handkerchief. Yesterday's heat had lingered through the previous night and intensified in the early morning.

She could hardly be called a pretty girl, he thought. Yet she had a certain freshness about her. There was something about her that he should be able to remember, but couldn't. Oh, well. It will probably come to him sometime later.

Then, more significantly, she said, "I saw Mr. Wilson on the campus several months ago. Is he joining the faculty?"

"I don't know, Dolores. Do you know him?"

"No, but my brother told me about him. He went to St. George's. He said that Mr. Wilson is a very likable person and he gave high grades, but if you want to learn anything, stay out of his classes. Well, I'm almost late for my class. Have a good day, Dr. Boudreaux."

"You, too. Miss — er — Pryer."

An idea had started to shape in Henry's mind. When he reached his office he said to Prisco. "Will you try to set up an appointment with Mr. André Wilson. This is his phone number."

The idea continued to grow. He went into the basement where the old records of St. George's were still stored, awaiting instruction for their disposal from Brother Benedict. After twenty minutes of digging into them, he came upon the faculty files. He extracted the files of Professors Wilson and Schaefer and took them up to his office.

"Matt, you know how difficult it has been to recruit suitable associate professors. Well, what do you think of this idea: recruit more assistant professors from the ranks of our own instructors. People like Prisco."

"Yes, Henry, you're right. The lack of prestige a new college offers, the insecurity involved in a new institution, especially an experimental institution, our emphasis on teaching rather than research, all make us unattractive to most experienced teachers. Most of the applications we get are from retired men and women, too set in their ways to adjust to a new approach. Or young people nobody else wants."

"Why would they apply for our positions, knowing that we have a radically different approach to instructing the young."

"I think it's because they are in financial difficulties. When they became sixty-five they qualified fully for pensions and for social security benefits. But if they had continued to teach, they would have lost much of their social security payments, so in effect that would amount to a deep cut in income. Once a person reached the age of seventy, however, he is entitled to his full social security benefits regardless of the size of his salary. So some try to return to the labor market. But many colleges will not hire them. So they flock to those that will. Hence, all the unsuitable applications we get. Unsuitable because of their inflexibility. Pretending to be flexible but determined to do things their own way once they have a contract. What have they got to lose? We give them a two-semester contract. They coast for two semesters, pick up forty thousand dollars, and if we kick them out as unproductive, or unsuitable, or inflexible, they're still forty thousands ahead of the game."

Henry said, "I once heard a college dean say that about a third of his teachers were very good, a third average and a third poor. Would you agree?"

Simmons thought for a while, then said "Yes, I suppose that would be correct in just about any institution. But don't forget that by emphasizing teaching over research, we have higher teaching standards. I won't settle for that. My goal is eighty percent outstanding, ten percent average and ten percent ineffective, with the ineffective on the way out at the first opportunity."

"So what do we do, Matt?"

"I think we should stick with the idea of recruiting assistant professors from our best instructors."

"But you said — and I agree with you — that it usually takes five years to make a Ph.D. into a teacher."

"Yes, but sometimes there are exceptions?"

"Do you have such an exception in mind?"

"I do. Martin."

Martin was delighted with the continuity. He could just continue where he had left off, only on a higher level. Instead of helping professors with their work, he would be teaching on his own.

The salary increase would come in handy, too. From ten thousand dollars per semester to fifteen. Forty-five thousand dollars a year and an apartment rent-free close to Manhattan. He and his wife could even put aside something as a down-payment on a house; Dr. Boudreaux did mention the possibility of promotion to associate professor with another fifteen-thousand-dollar-a-year raise within the next two years.

The reaction of several of the other instructors was, understandably, jealousy. Some became very cool toward Martin; others covered their hostility under the guise of exaggerated friendship and hoped to learn somehow his formula for success. Still others couldn't care less; they had never intended to remain in teaching after they got their Ph.D.'s.

"I'd say its a bit premature, Henry," said Robert Chang. "Academically speaking, these young people are still not dry behind the ears. In most cases, it takes five years teaching experience to make a teacher."

"But we have people on our faculty with no teaching experience at all."

"Yes, but none of these young people is on his own. In a sense, each is only a teacher's helper under the close supervision of a veteran teacher."

The remaining associate professorship remained vacant throughout the summer semester. This meant that four of the full professors had to go on over-time at no additional pay for four hot months.

Now he remembered. He was returning from Seton Hall, driving down South Orange Avenue. Traffic was heavy. It was right after crossing Old Short Hills Road when he noticed the girl in the red convertible riding his bumper. Too close. It worried him. He slowed down in order to force her to pass, but every attempt she made to get into the center lane was cut off by motorists already there. She persisted. She scared the hell out of him with her persistence. Finally, when they reached the Eisenhower Parkway, they were stopped by a red light, her car finally in the center lane and right next to his.

He called out to her, "Young lady, the way you drive is hazardous to your health."

Not bothering to look in his direction, she replied scornfully, "Fuck you, old man."

"No, thanks, young lady That would be hazardous to *my* health."

Yes, that young lady was Miss Pryer.

SIXTEEN

Two August-hot days later André Wilson sat, sweating, in Henry's outer office, his mind racing while he waited to be invited in. He was a reasonable man, he told himself. He wasn't greedy. All he wanted was a year's salary to pay off the debts he had incurred during his two semesters of unemployment, and another year's salary to tide him over until he found another job. That wasn't much to ask. Another man would take the racist bastards to the cleaners. He never liked Henry Boudreaux anyway. He certainly would never want to teach for that conceited man. Or that Uncle Tom, Matthew Simmons, either.

But what if Henry offered him a job instead of a settlement. He guessed he'd have to take it and make the best of it until he could do better. He'd still insist on that year's back pay. Strange how nobody had offered him a job during the past year. Perhaps some of them didn't like Black professors.

Or old professors. Especially old Black professors, especially those with no Ph.D.'s. Hadn't they ever heard of equal-opportunity employment?

Meanwhile, in his office Henry was stalling until Dean Simmons could complete his lecture and join them in his office. This was a job for both of them.

The buzzer of the intercom sounded. "Yes?"

"Mr. Wilson is here to see you, Dr. Boudreaux. And Dr. Simmons."

His face solemn, the dean entered, following André Wilson, who exuded confidence as he seated himself on the chair at Henry's right.

"Glad we could get together, Henry," he said. "I knew you'd see it my way."

Henry did not return his smile. "And what way is that André."

André was confused. Then he smiled again. Foxy old Boudreaux. Up to his old tricks. What this maneuvering was all about was the terms of the settlement. Like any other administrator, he wanted to settle as cheaply as possible. Well, two could play that game.

Henry continued. "When Brother Benedict evacuated these premises, he left behind, for the time being, all the records of defunct St. George's College. Including your file as an assistant professor. I had a look at those records."

André's face became grim as Henry continued, "I once had a student tell me that he did not mind a good teacher who gave low grades or a bad teacher who gave high grades. What he couldn't stand was a bad teacher who gave low grades. Well, André, he'd love you. You were a bad teacher who gave exceedingly high grades. I would never want such a teacher on my faculty."

André was furious. He jumped from his chair and bent over Henry's desk, screaming, "Who the hell do you think you are? You violated my right to privacy. I'll sue you. You had no right to go digging into those records. You are not my supervisor!"

It was Henry's turn to smile, saying, "I'm glad you feel that way, André."

Puzzled, André turned to face Matthew who also smiled, shrugged his shoulders, and said: "I'm sure you realize, Mr. Wilson, that you can't have it both ways. Either Santa Sophia is St. George's operating under another name, or it isn't. If it is, Dr. Boudreaux has every right to go into those records and use the damning evidence he found there to deny you a contract. You remember, of course, that you had no tenure at St. George's. On the other hand, if St. George's went out of existence and Santa Sophia is a new college, then Henry owes you nothing since you're just another job applicant. Now which is it? Obviously, either way you lose."

For a moment they thought that André was going to strike Simmons. Then it seemed like he was going to have a stroke. Finally, he growled at Dr. Simmons, "You goddamned Uncle Tom," and rushed out of the office.

For a long time Henry was speechless. When his mind returned on track he said to Simmons, "Excuse me, Matt. There's something else I have to do while I'm still on a roll."

"**Dr. Schaefer?** Dr. Boudreaux of Santa Sophia College calling. Dr. Schaefer, we have been conducting investigations and I'm sure you'd be interested in what we found out. About you. You were offered associate professorships by two universities in Northern New Jersey and three more in Manhattan. Is that correct?"

Silence.

"You turned them all down, even though the salary scale was in some cases considerably higher than either St. George's or Santa Sophia could pay.

"Now don't hang up on me, Schaefer. It would be to your disadvantage if you did not hear me out. OK?

"As I see it, Dr. Schaefer, although you are a brilliant scientist, you really don't want to teach undergraduates. You want to confine yourself to research but you need someone to support you, and you need someone to pay the cost of your esoteric research. Since you have not been able to find a sponsor in government or business, legal extortion of two years' salary from Santa Sophia seemed like a good thing.

"Well, it won't work, and here's why. I have in my possession records of your poor performance as a teacher at St. George's College that will prove my case."

Schaefer replied, dryly, "Not admissible as evidence in a court of law."

"What if they're not? I can get a dozen of your former students to testify as to your ineffective teaching. And I can get Brother Benedict to testify that he was not going to renew your two-year contract. The demise of St. George's did not affect your teaching career because you would have been out of a job even if it had remained open. Hence, if the court found that Santa Sophia was St. George's operating under another name — and that is doubtful — you still would not be legally entitled to a job with us. Now, Dr. Schaefer, do we still go to court? Dr. Schaefer? Hello!"

It was a hot day for a man of his age to be pushing a lawn mower, even an electric lawn mower. Henry was also baby-sitting David. The five-year-old had his own toy lawn mower which he pushed vigorously, although, of course, it did not cut grass or children. This did not seem to matter to the boy, as long as he could be with his *pipère*. Lying in the shade of a twenty-foot evergreen tree, Max kept both of them under surveillance.

Twenty-five years ago Henry had bought a live Christmas tree, four feet tall, and almost surprising them when they planted it in the front yard, it lived. Every Christmas season they had decorated it with ornaments and lights until it became too tall for them to reach. Now it simply stood there reminding them of how long they had lived in Eunice.

There were other reminders. Three maples that marked the boundary line between the ten feet of town property next to the street and land owned by the Boudreauxs had been planted from seed. Yes, seed. Henry had planted the maple seeds on the south side of his house, close to the foundation. Within three or four years he had saplings taller than he. Three of these he planted on the property line. Now they were even taller than the evergreen, and two feet in diameter. Too bad their innumerable seeds made such a mess in the front yard every spring.

Henry used an electric lawn mower because gasoline mowers hated him, starting only after much coaxing and then conking out at the slightest provocation. Dragging behind a hundred and fifty feet of heavy electric cord, he admitted, was a nuisance. Once he ran at if you run over the cord; he never did it again.

"I have an appointment with the president."
The student-receptionist knew the rolly-polly young man standing before her. In fact, probably everyone of Santa Sophia's students knew him. Dudley Donovan — for that was his name — saw to that. He was the kind of person who had to have somebody's attention at all times. It did not seem to matter to him whether that attention was favorable or unfavorable.

"Go right in, Dudley," she said.

As if I didn't have enough trouble, Henry thought as he looked up and saw who his visitor was.

"Good afternoon, Mr. Donovan. Have a seat. What can I do for you?"

One point for me, thought Donovan. He calls every other student by his first name.

"Dr. Boudreaux, I'm here to present a petition on behalf of the majority of the students of Santa Sophia."

He handed the president an official-looking document. Henry turned several pages to reach the signatures on the final page. He estimated that there were between twenty and twenty-five signatures. I thought so, he said to himself.

He proceeded to read the signatures, some of which were illegible. Deliberately so? A professor usually does not remember all the students he has taught in a lengthy career. About eight thousands, in Henry's case. Certain categories are remembered: those with brilliant minds, the creative, those

with little ability but great determination, and, of course, the
neurotics, the pains in the ass. For one reason or another,
Henry recognized every legible name on the list.

"I would estimate, Mr. Donovan, that the names on this list
represent more like a fifth of our students than a majority.
Yet you present this petition as coming from a majority."

Dudley compressed his lips. "I do, Dr. Boudreaux. Of
course, many of the students are too cowardly to sign any petition."

"I commend you for *your* courage, Mr. Donovan. I'll have
copies of your petition sent to every member of the Board of
Trustees. We shall then discuss the matter at our next regular
meeting, and I shall let you know our decision. Now is there
anything else?"

Dudley obviously was surprised. He had been prepared for
a fight, but the president had robbed him of his ammunition.
Looking disappointed, he left to plan his next move.

For the next three weeks Santa Sophia ran smoothly.
Student and faculty complaints which reached its president
were few and inconsequential. Henry began to worry. There
must be trouble for us somewhere, probably just over the
horizon. He knew that he was right when the letter he received bore the intimidating return address of the Internal
Revenue Service. He summoned the bursar.

"This could ruin us, Saul. If they get away with it, Santa
Sophia could be driven out of business."

Saul could see that Henry was really worried.

Henry continued. "Here we are trying to keep the cost of
higher education within bounds and a few petty bureaucrats

are trying to destroy us. What is worse, they have the power to do so."

Saul had never seen him so worked up. "Slow down, Henry. Tell me exactly what the situation is."

Henry handed him the official letter in its intimidating envelope. "It seems that one of the auditors in our local office is claiming that our students are required to report as income the value of their labor on campus. In other words, that the law requires them to calculate the value of their service at the going rate, report this amount on their Forms 1040, and pay the additional tax. Then they could fill out additional forms and get a student loan guaranteed by the federal government. But that way everybody loses — the students, the taxpayers, everybody but the bureaucrats. Now what can we do about this preposterous situation?"

Saul thought for a while then said, "I really don't know, Henry, but I see what you mean. If we can't beat this arbitrary action, its consequences could ruin us and a lot of other private colleges as well. To begin, we would have to increase tuition to pay the additional costs of bookkeeping and auditing. That would make us less attractive to incoming freshmen. Then the additional income taxes paid by our students would, in effect, add further to the cost of their education. That might be enough to cancel out any financial benefits they might derive by attending Santa Sophia or any other school operating on similar principles."

"But what can we do? The courts tend to favor IRS, and even if we win, the cost of the litigation would break our financial backs." Henry's plea was desperate.

"Easy, Henry. It may not come to litigation."

Saul wished he had the confidence he was trying to instill in his friend.

January 21, 1993.

Dear Son,

As you know, I don't believe in birthday presents or Christmas presents or Anniversary presents. Advertising people have taken over our lives, making gifts psychologically mandatory on an ever increasing number of occasions. In addition to Mothers' Day and Fathers' Day, we now have Grandparents' Day, Secretary's Day and Boss's Day.

To me, items given on those days are not gifts but entitlements. Gifts are freely given. Gifts are from the heart. Gifts spring from friendship, from love, from paternal devotion. The little item I am sending you is to be regarded as a gift, not a birthday present.

Love,

Dad

He checked the monitor for typos and misspelled words. He had never been a good speller. Corrections were made and the printer turned on. He hit the print keys on the computer and the laser printer hummed.

He addressed the envelope to Pat's Manhattan apartment. Then he remembered that Pat was playing in a road company in San Francisco, so he threw the addressed envelope into the waste basket, made the change of address and printed another envelope, stamped it and put the letter inside.

Now, if only he could remember to get someone to set his digital watch for him, he would no longer have to deduct an hour every time he wanted to tell time. Ah, technology.

SEVENTEEN

Henry was not reassured by Saul's comforting words about the Internal Revenue Service. As he saw it, due to a fluke in American institutions, an innocent tax payer has less chance of prevailing against an arbitrary IRS ruling than a habitual criminal has of beating the rap on a legal technicality. Even those known to be professional criminals are regarded as innocent by the law until proven guilty, but it's up to the taxpayer to prove, at his own expense, that the tax collectors are wrong.

And, ironically, even if Santa Sophia could prevail in a court of law, the cost of doing so could be so heavy that the school would probably be bankrupted. It was a no-win situation. Perhaps O'Malley could pull a few strings in favor of justice.

This year's presentation of English 302 was a production of *The Merchant of Venice*. It had been many years since Henry had read the Shakespearian play, and he had never seen it performed on the stage, so when Saul and his wife, Beatrice, invited Henry and Grace to go with them, neither hesitated to accept. Their first impression was, those kids are good actors. As the play progressed, however, they became increasingly embarrassed by the anti-Semitic dialogue. Before the final curtain Henry felt like hiding under his seat. Saul merely said, "I think those kids have given us one helluva performance, don't you, Henry?"

"Yes, I know, Saul. So why do I feel so rotten?"

Saul smiled at his friend and replied, "Because those kids have given one helluva performance."

"What's this rumor about a problem with IRS? I thought that as a non-profit corporation the school was free from harassment by those people."

Henry had met Ray Donato in the corridor. Ray looked a bit under the weather but he insisted that there was nothing wrong with him.

"A bureaucratic maneuver," Henry replied. "Those people have to convince their supervisors that they are earning their salaries. And would you want to tangle with the high-priced accountants and lawyers of a billion-dollar corporation if you were in their shoes?"

"So it's just a matter of filling out a few forms."

"I hope so, Ray, but you can never tell."

Grace was in the living room watching "her" show on television. In his study Henry slumped in his easy chair, the one which fitted the contours of his body so well that he felt uncomfortable sitting anywhere else. The TV set was turned on to "his" program; an open book was on his lap. At his feet, Max lay stretched out on the brown and green shag carpet, taking up half the room. Max liked the carpet because it was soft, and because it smelled of his master. Henry liked it because it didn't show the countless long hairs which Max was constantly discarding. When commercials came on, the man returned to his reading, since most commercials did not interest him. On the half-hour his show went off, and he darkened the tube by remote control. He let his thoughts stray, first to Santa Sophia where he had more problems than he wanted to think about, then to St. George's and Joseph White, from whom he had inherited most of those problems.

Grace had tried a new cleaning woman, and she too had turned out to be unsatisfactory. It was a matter of attitude. The woman had started out well, earning the fifty dollars in cash which she received for half a day's work. Then she began to reduce the time she worked, from four hours to three and a half, then three hours, down to two and a half. At first, the work still seemed to get done, then it became obvious that this was not the case. Then she wanted an additional ten dollars for cleaning the oven and still more for the bathroom floor. When she was refused, she simply quit. Henry had to resist the urge to say to his wife, "I told you so."

Joseph, the European, had been surprised to find that the Boudreauxs did not employ domestic help. He found it even more shocking when he saw the master of the household, a professor no less, on his knees, scrubbing his own floors and then dusting his own furniture.

Henry explained. "Ordinarily, we can't afford it, but when I was accidentally burned and Grace had to work long hours we tried hiring occasional help. It didn't work, because they wouldn't. A few good people did come our way. An Arab woman who had to quit because she became ill, a Black woman who had to help her husband when his business ran into a cash flow problem, and an Italian-born woman who was willing to be my servant if I became her servant and picked her up and brought her home although she usually drove her own car.

"So we face it. The servant is obsolete as far as the American middle class is concerned. And the clean-up teams which clean offices have not expanded their services to meet the needs of families. Cleaning offices is much more profitable and has far fewer headaches than cleaning homes."

Joseph couldn't decide whether this trend was socially beneficial or harmful.

Henry had seldom driven a car in Manhattan. The Bronx and Staten Island, yes, but almost never in Manhattan. He didn't have the nerve. This explained his presence on a New York bound bus. Of course, he did not object to the half-fare rate for senior citizens during the non-rush hours. These days he seldom went into the city. The pace was too tiring.

But he could never read on a bus. On a train, yes, but never on a bus. So he would watch the passing scene, or rather the scene they were passing. Past the Newark Airport, to the turnpike, off the turnpike, to the approach to the Lincoln Tunnel. Today he had made the mistake of sitting near the front which meant that the press of exiting passengers prevented him from getting off until everybody else was off. He strained his aching neck looking for an opportunity to break into the solid phalanx of retreating passengers, but none came.

Off at last, he headed to the men's room. Bus rides did that to him. The Seventh Avenue subway took him to West 14th Street where a local train took him one stop beyond. There passengers were, for the most part, shabbily dressed, people of limited means, paying more than a dollar for a ride which a few years ago had cost a nickel. Graffiti "decorated" every wall, including the maps that helped him find his way through this ugly, dirty labyrinth.

Pat met him at the subway exit nearest St. Vincent's hospital. "Good to see you, Dad," he said.

"Thanks for your invitation, Son," his father replied.

They walked through the streets of The Village. Some areas had a reputation for violence, but so far this area had been spared.

"There are some advantages to living here," Pat observed. "You learn which blocks of which streets to avoid. I made reservations for lunch at Brigitte's."

What surprised Henry about the restaurant was its size. He doubted whether more than a dozen customers could squeeze into the place at any one time. Only those with reservations were admitted, but once seated they did not have to order. All of that had been taken care of in advance. The food was excellent.

As they were being seated by Brigitte herself, Pat said,

"Dad, I have good news for you. I have been cast in a minor role of a major play. We go into rehearsal next week. Without the money you and Mom gave me, I never could have done it. I'm really sorry about our — differences."

"Forget it, Son," he replied. "You did have a point. The concept of an education should be extended to include an internship in certain professions. Such as yours."

His son protested. "Yes, but that money you gave me. It must have been your entire take-home pay for your first year at Santa Sophia. I'm determined to pay you back every penny."

It was the father's turn to protest. "I don't need it. I don't want it. And, by the way, I'm giving your brother my second year's salary to bail him out of hock. It's important to him and his family that they start out without undue indebtedness. Otherwise, he may never get off the treadmill."

The tiny theater was within easy walking distance. It had about three hundred seats and no stage. Theirs was in the second row, which meant that the actors performed practically on top of the audience. It was that indestructible mini-musical, "The Fantastiks." Henry loved it, but then Pat knew that because his father was always playing its recordings.

"Technically, I don't think it would be called a heart attack, Ray," Henry said, "but it could have killed him just the same. You see, Saul has a chronic atrial fibrillation. It's a tendency toward irregular heartbeats. In Saul's case, the problem starts in the upper chamber of the heart. It is chronic, and it could be caused by a valve problem or an inadequate supply of blood to his heart due to the clogging of his arteries.

It makes his heart beat very quickly. A slight one might last for only four or five minutes, and then he could go about his business. Occasionally, it is a matter of an hour or so, leaving him so debilitated that he has to go to bed early and take a sleeping pill to assure himself of a complete night's rest. Then he's OK in the morning. As long as he stays with his medication."

He did not mention Saul's words. "My cardiologist blames it on fatigue. He has ordered complete rest for a few months. If it gets any worse, Henry, I'll have to have a pacemaker installed. Then I'll have to stay out of your kitchen with its microwave oven."

Ray seemed very sympathetic. Old people relate to other old people in matters of the heart.

"And this one was even worse than usual?" he asked.

"Much worse," Henry continued. "You see, as I said, fatigue exacerbates the problem. Saul could not sleep for worrying over our financial problems and trying to come up with a solution. At five o'clock he got up to go to the bathroom and collapsed at the foot of his bed. The ambulance got there in four minutes. He woke up in an emergency room of Morristown Memorial hospital where he heard the words 'possible heart attack' and passed out again. The next time he regained consciousness he was in the cardiac care room tied up to all those machines. The doctor in charge told Beatrice that it was improbable that he would live, so she'd better notify the family. Saul had his eyes closed but he heard him and resigned himself to death.

"He told me all this three days later, when I was allowed to see him for a few minutes by saying that I was his brother.

'But I fooled them, Henry. You can have your EKG's. They can only measure a physical condition. But no machine ever invented can measure the determination of a tough old Jew like me.' "

Ray smiled.

"Henry, you don't know how good this makes me feel. I knew he'd lick it. I just knew he'd lick it. Of course, he'll be disabled for a long time, so we've temporarily lost a bursar. But we still have our friend, and that's what's important."

Ray wondered if it would be in bad taste to ask who would assume the job of bursar. Henry read his thoughts.

"He's even arranged for his daughter's accounting firm to take over the duties of bursar. Alicia's also a C.P.A., you know."

"Yes, I know."

They both knew that this would mean an added financial burden for Santa Sophia; they both were ashamed of thinking in financial terms when the life of a friend, in immediate danger of death, had been spared.

Henry, who loved summer, made the transition from warm weather clothing to cool weather clothing reluctantly. It was like saying *Adieu* to an old friend you weren't sure you'd ever see again. His baseball cap was replaced by a French beret, his Bermuda shorts by a warm-up suit, and his Spanish straw shoes (which are made of plastic these days), by a pair of moccasins called "boat shoes." He loved moccasins, although he hated the way their leather shoestrings were constantly being untied by the ghosts of Indians long dead.

EIGHTEEN

The message Henry found on his fax machine had no signature. His first reaction was one of resentment; how dare people intrude this way. Once he had read the message, however, his resentment was quickly replaced by curiosity.

Don't trust Dennis; he's out to screw you.

The anonymous author had to be someone in the inner office of Charles O'Malley. Perhaps one of Henry's former students. An enemy of Dennis? An enemy of Charles? Regardless, he would no longer trust either of them. Perhaps he never had.

He was picking up the buzzing phone as Robert Chang entered the room. Robert would have to wait. Clearly, Henry was angry. The party at the other end was doing most of the talking, but Henry did get in a few words edgewise. "But these are not employees in the usual sense of the words. They are students who are learning everyday skills which few people have mastered. They are honing these skills by their experience. . . . Then I guess you'll just have to hold your hearing."

Robert waited for his friend to speak. He waited a long time. Finally, Henry said, "Can you beat that!"

"What?"

"Do you know Donovan?"

"Pay-attention-to-me Donovan? Ego-maniacal Donovan? Everybody knows *that* Donovan. And most students seem to dislike him."

"Such people are usually disliked," Henry replied. "Well, he came in here last month with a petition signed by ten or fifteen malcontents. I think I disappointed him when I told him I would place the matter before the Board of Trustees, rather than rejecting it outright. Did you get your copy?"

"I got my copy. That's what I'm here to discuss with you. Some of his demands are preposterous. All of them seem to give power to him."

"And his friends. They certainly would make it more difficult to operate this college efficiently."

Henry mopped his face with his handkerchief. "The very thing we're trying to avoid. It isn't that I'm insensitive to the needs of the students. I have been developing that sensitivity for forty years. I just can't let the psychological needs of every nut who comes along get between us and what we are trying to do."

Robert nodded, understanding, "Don't you think, Henry, that the average student, inarticulate though he may be, disapproves of Donovan and his ilk?"

Henry wasn't sure. "I'd say 'yes' with qualifications. In the first place, the average student could not possibly be fully aware of all its implications. It's like the student revolt in the 1960's. Those students had a lot to revolt against. You remember how the power of professors at that time was absolute. And you remember how some professors abused that power? Well, the kids had a lot of valid complaints, but some of them used this as an excuse to create chaos."

Robert laughed. "Yes. I remember the demand that grades be abolished. I was the first to join them in supporting that point of view. I told them that if we eliminated grades, I would not have to grade examination papers, or tests, or term papers. Eliminate grades and you eliminate half of my work, and the unpleasant half at that. By now I was being cheered like a winning basketball coach. Then I added, 'But if we eliminate grades, I don't write letters of recommendation for you when you go for job interviews.'

"The cheering stopped. Suddenly, it was very quiet when I said, 'I cannot supply a prospective employer with information I do not have, but that's no skin off my nose. I already have an employer.' The quiet was replaced by the sound of a thousand bees buzzing around a hive. That was the last I ever heard of that proposal."

Finally, Henry was smiling.

It was Saturday and Henry was pleased at the thought that for a few hours he could ignore the problems of a college president. Then his daughter-in-law drove up, picked up his wife and dropped off his teen-age granddaughter. Girl-children always baffled Henry, since he had never had a daughter to bring up, so he never knew what to expect from his grand-daughter except one surprise after another.

Today was no different. Her mother and grandmother had no sooner driven away when Hélène began to clean the kitchen. Later, from his study, he could hear the vacuum cleaner hum over the carpet of the living- and dining-room areas. Hélène had frequently cleaned up the kitchen, but cleaning the living room was something new. "What's going on?" he asked as she unplugged the silent sweeper to move it to another room.

"I'm earning money," she replied. "My Christmas shopping left me broke."

Since she had bought him a pair of expensive fleece-lined moccasins for Christmas, he felt guilty of contributing to her financial predicament.

"Take a break, Hélène. Let me do some of this," he said.

"No, *Pipère*. I have to earn my way," she insisted.

Perhaps that's not a bad idea, he thought, and returned to his study where he had papers to shuffle. In a few minutes she was there to clean his study, and he wondered if he should retreat with his paperwork to the living room or to the kitchen, or better still, perhaps, to his office on the campus.

"Nana said that the going rate for cleaning ladies is a hundred dollars a day. She is paying me fifty dollars for a half day."

She learns quickly, he thought.

"That's twice what I could earn at a fast-food place and the work is easier. So why are cleaning women so hard to get?"

Henry put his papers aside, lay back in his easy chair and slipped back into the role of educator.

"In the first place, Americans look down on servants. They regard this work as degrading. Some employers display this attitude openly, which is humiliating to those they employ.

"Then there's danger of being blamed for something you didn't do. A vase is broken by the cat, or a piece of jewelry is misplaced. You were there so you are suspected. When something goes wrong, it's only human to absolve one's self of blame by blaming someone else. Servants make perfect fall guys because they are there."

The girl talked and listened without interrupting her dusting.

"My mom says that it is a good thing for me to baby-sit and clean the house because every woman should know housekeeping skills. Miss Adrianna, our English teacher, says it molds women into stereotypes. It brainwashes us into accepting a role assigned to us by male chauvinists. Who's right?"

Henry was beginning to feel hungry. Well, there were several casseroles in the freezer ready for the microwave oven.

"They're both right, honey. A young girl should master all the domestic skills so that she can take care of herself and her family when she gets one. And a young boy should master the same skills because it is unlikely that he will be able to pay someone else for this service in today's market. In other words, *ma chère*, there's nothing a woman does that a man can't do. Well, almost nothing. I can change a diaper as well as any woman.

"On the other hand, no woman should ever let anybody else — not even women libbers — tell her who she is. It's every woman's prerogative to arrive at and protect her own identity."

Then it occurred to him that with his arthritic fingers he

would be reluctant to pick up a baby. But that was beside the point.

Hélène again turned on the vacuum cleaner, its noise ending the conversation. She was quite secure in her own self-image. The way she saw it, once she became a teenager, she was no longer a child. She was an adult, although her mother didn't always see it that way. Well, she had a good mother compared to those of other kids so she'd be patient with her. Of course, once she got her driver's license, no one could possibly dispute her claim to adult status.

This time Saul's daughter, Alicia, did not phone; she came over to Henry's office. Bad news, he thought; Alicia usually phoned. Bad news it was.

"Our financial situation is critical, Henry," she said. "Three of your most important creditors are talking tough. They demand to be paid within the week. We only have enough money to pay one of them. Worse still, we can't meet the faculty payroll which is due next Friday. Tuition for next semester isn't being paid. We have to get more credit and we have to get it fast."

She thought that Henry looked frightened, desperate. He was. He no longer thought in terms of break-even but of survival. "I was afraid of that, Alicia. It means that I'll have to crawl back to O'Malley."

Alicia was not very hopeful. "I was afraid of that."

Did Henry detect a note of hopelessness in her voice? Or was it but an echo of his own fears?

"If only we didn't have such rotten luck, like the kind of expenses nobody could have anticipated."

She could only say, "A professional administrator would say that he would have anticipated them."

"Perhaps he would be correct," Henry agreed.

"Perhaps. But I doubt it. I am beginning to see a pattern in our so-called bad luck. As if someone had planned the whole thing in advance and executed it, step by step."

Henry wanted to reject the idea. "But who would have a motive to do such a thing"

"If we knew that," Alicia replied as she got up to leave, "we would be well on the way to solving our problem."

A very nervous college president waited for Dennis to return his phone call. Without additional credit from Charles O'Malley, Santa Sophia could no longer operate. Finally, he called again, risking the wrath of Dennis's secretary. There was a discernible chill in her voice.

"Mr. Velez is out of town, and I don't know when he'll be back. Sorry, sir. That's all I can tell you."

Henry was getting desperate. In spite of his explicit instructions to deal only with Dennis — in other words, don't bother O'Malley; he can't be bothered with trivia — he decided to go directly to the boss. Then he realized that he had neither an office address nor a phone number where O'Malley could be reached.

It took a while before his research produced the phone numbers of all six of O'Malley's companies. The first five he dialed brushed him off. "Mr. O'Malley is not in." How do you cope with that? Suddenly he remembered that his meetings with O'Malley had always been in a restaurant instead of his office. He had wondered if this had any significance.

Now he feared it had.

The sixth call offered hope. If Dr. Boudreaux would leave his phone number, they would try to get in touch with Mr. O'Malley and call him back.

"I'm not seeing anybody for the time being, Steve. Unless it's somebody on the Board. Henry then paced the floor, waiting an eternity until a telephone's ringing jarred him back to the present.

"Dr. Boudreaux?"

"Yes."

"This is Mr. Jenkins of the National Labor Relations Board."

For a moment Henry forgot all his other troubles. What could they possible want with us? He soon found out.

"A number of your teachers and student-employees have formed a union and they have petitioned us to conduct an election to determine whether or not this union should represent your faculty as its collective bargaining agent."

The bureaucrat allowed his squirming victim enough time to absorb the impact of the message, then continued.

"Of course, Dr. Boudreaux, you could avoid the trouble and expense of an election by simply recognizing the union. You would then notify us of that fact. Negotiations could then begin on a contract."

Absurd, Henry thought. The senior faculty was clearly "management," and could not join a union. The junior faculty was transient, so he felt certain that most of them expected to leave after a year or two. His first impulse was to call for an election and take his chances. But that would take money and

Santa Sophia had no money. What could he do? Stall. At least long enough to sort things out.

How do you sort things out when your mind is completely befuddled. You don't. He was not scheduled to teach any classes that day. He'd take the rest of the afternoon off and enjoy the sunshine. Gardening always helped. It made sense when nothing else did. You planted seeds, you cultivated the plants and you eat the fruits of your labor. He'd work in his garden. That's what he'd do.

"Steve," he said through his inter-com; "I'm leaving for the day."

He had his beret on when the phone rang. The hell with it, he said to himself. Then he remembered that O'Malley's office had promised to call back. It was O'Malley's office. Mr. O'Malley could not be reached. Would he try again next week?"

NINETEEN

On January 17, 1993, Raymon Donato dropped dead of a stroke. His students knew that something was wrong. Obviously ill, he seemed to be trying to hang on until the end of the class period. He didn't make it, dismissing his class ten minutes early and walking slowly and painfully to his office. There he passed out, falling soundlessly to the carpet. He never regained consciousness.

Henry took it hard, helping Angela, the widow, as best he could. So did Ray's sons and daughters, and their sons and daughters, even those who lived in Atlanta and Chicago who seldom saw their grandfather. It could be said that Ray was his best friend, but Henry had several "best friends," including the one who had killed himself. Since Santa Sophia had become a reality, even before that, Ray and Bob Chang had been his right and left hands, and now one of them was taken from him, permanently and without warning.

Without warning? Wasn't the accumulation of the years warning enough? At our age the eagle of Death always roosts on our shoulders. We can't shoo him away, so we might as well make friends with him. The same God who invented birth invented death, and Henry could think of no way of improving on either.

And wasn't he being selfish, egocentric to think of Ray's death in terms of his own personal loss? Yes, he was. But wasn't that always the case? The dead people we loved are out of harm's way, and what hurts us is the vacuum that remains in our own lives after they have gone.

And what a loss. To lose a close friend can be worse than losing a brother. We are drawn to our friends because of a common interest, a mutual respect. This is not necessarily true in the case of our brothers. Our friends are usually near by, but in today's society our brothers are usually many miles away. Friends, by definition, are usually there when you need them. Brothers seldom are.

Statistically, Henry felt that he had about ten more years to live. Even if he were still alive by 1999, he'd probably be too feeble of body, and perhaps of mind as well, to do anything worthwhile. With apologies to Ira Gershwin, who calls that living?

The wake was at Burroughs, Kohr and Dangler in Madison. Henry was all too familiar with that funeral home since he seemed to be going to a lot of wakes there in recent years. It's the price we pay for out-living our friends, for being sur-vivors, he said to himself. Well, eventually it would be his turn. He wondered if the entire student body of Santa Sophia would attend his wake, as seemed to be Ray's case. It wouldn't make any difference to him. Wakes are for the living; the dead are untouched by them, he told himself.

The funeral was on the following Monday. The weather was so cold that Henry wondered why the bone-chilling rain was not sleet or snow. The interior of St. Vincent's Church had been renovated since Henry had last been there. It was redesigned as a theater-in-the-round, and he hated it. Ray had hated it too, but there was nothing he could do about it. A parish is not a democracy. And the use of English instead of age-old Latin in the ritual. Something else Henry had a hard time accepting.

Henry drove the fourth car behind Angie's limousine, leaving most of the mourners still at the church. Across Main Street to Central Avenue, then through Florham Park and East Hanover, by way of Ridgedale Avenue, streets he had driven over so many times with Ray, and often with Max seated upright in the back seat like a chauffeur-driven gentleman. As they approached the Gate of Heaven Cemetery in East Hanover, he could no longer hold back his tears.

"Why did you have to go and leave me, you goddamned Dago?" he mumbled.

His wife, Grace, pretended that she neither saw nor heard him.

That night, trying in vain to get some sleep, Henry could not help but recall how different Ray's funeral was from Joseph's. Immediately after the "accident," Henry had been contacted by Joseph's lawyer. As instructed, he had had the half-charred remains cremated, and claimed the ashes. He then chartered a light plane at the Morristown Airport and flew out to sea. There he scattered into the wind the ashes that had once been his tragic friend. That was the way Joseph had wanted it. Henry's face-off with Brother Sophos had followed immediately.

"Dr. White devoted thirty unselfish years to the students of St. George's College," he had argued. "You should at the very least hold a memorial Mass for the happy repose of his soul."

Brother Sophos was trying to be patient with an insubordinate man he really did not like. "Dr. White was not a Catholic. In fact, he seemed to practice no religion at all. I do not feel that a Mass for him would be appropriate."

Henry was disappointed, but not surprised.

"Then why not a non-denominational memorial service to show our appreciation of him?"

Brother Sophos's patience came to an abrupt end.

"This is a Catholic school, Henry, or do I have to remind you? A non-denominational service would not only be inappropriate but sacrilegious. And don't forget your part in his cremation."

Henry was angry enough to spit in his face, but he knew he could get nowhere with this fanatic. He left without saying another word.

TWENTY

"I can't wait. Tell me about it."

Patricia stood in the doorway, ignoring the student-receptionist who was trying to keep her out.

"Good news," Henry said, smiling. "Internal Revenue has had a change of heart, if "heart" is the right word. The value of a student's labor in lieu of tuition will not be subject to taxation. They now accept our contention that the work these students do is also a learning experience and part of our educational process."

Patricia was too excited to sit down. "Of course, it was ridiculous. This sort of thing would cost the federal government more money in administrative costs than the amount of taxes collected. Like the taxes on our Social Security checks. That's obvious. I can't see who would benefit from such a policy. Certainly not the students or tax payers."

"Only the paper shufflers," Henry replied. "Not to mention

the additional headaches for us and for our students."

Patricia was still too excited to sit. "What I'd like to know, Henry, is how did you pull it off?"

Henry savored his victory. "Well, I knew that as a small school we couldn't swing much weight. So I asked myself who else would be adversely affected by this ruling. The answer soon became apparent: every private college in this country. My next step was to call this to their bursars' attention in a convincing way. So I got on the telephone and called the bursars of every major private institution I could reach. It didn't take more than a few hours before I had made some powerful allies and perhaps even a few friends.

"My argument was that if our activity were taxable, so were a lot of theirs. Anyway, within forty-eight hours I got a call from the president of an ivy league university telling me not to worry, that he had been personally assured by someone high up in the ranks of IRS that they had nixed the whole idea, and that we'd be officially notified of this decision within a few days."

"That's wonderful news, Henry. Wonderful! But I wouldn't want to see your telephone bill."

The smile faded from his face. "Neither would I," he said.

Dr. Prisco dropped by immediately after the meeting, risking being regarded as a brown-noser. "I just had to tell you, Dr. Boudreaux. It was perfect. It couldn't have gone better. I was all prepared to put in my bit for the *status quo*, but I didn't have to. Another Assistant Professor did it for me, and he did it better than I could have. He started out with the theme of self-interest and he stuck with it all the way. First, what did they, the instructors and assistant professors, have to lose? Then what did they have to gain? It soon became apparent to even the soreheads that we had a lot more to lose than to gain by bringing a labor union into our situation. Finally, he asked that they vote "no union" because that would be in the best interest of all concerned. The vast majority did just that, as you'll see by the official report when it is issued."

The students, meanwhile, were debating the same topic, with Donovan leading the debate. "Don't you think it's inconsistent for Dr. Boudreaux to favor unionism for other colleges and universities, but oppose unionization for the student workers at Santa Sophia?"

There was a silent pause, then buzzing. Finally, a girl spoke up and asked, "How long do you expect to be on this campus, Dudley?"

For once he had nothing to say, so she answered her own question. "Another year, at most. And, I might add, the same is true for most of the assistant professors and instructors. Well, in my view a union exists to protect a worker committed to a life-long career. In the case of student-workers, it would hardly be worth the bother and the cost unless the professors turned into tyrants, and I haven't seen any signs of that.

"If Dudley had anything further to say, there was so much applause followed by so much chatter that nobody heard him. The vote was overwhelming in favor of no union, with only a handful of malcontents voting for a union."

The registrar was in an agitated state. "I just can't understand it. Half of our next group of freshmen have notified us that they would not be present for the orientation program. They changed their minds about coming to Santa Sophia, even though they had to forfeit half of their first semester's tuition which they had already paid. When I asked why, most of them simply said that they had decided to go somewhere else.

"When I finally got a straight answer from some of them they said that they had heard it on good authority that Santa Sophia was going bankrupt and it would soon close down."

Henry shook his head. "Good Lord, would you please give us a break. All I ask for is one good, trouble-free day. This morning it looked a lot like I was going to get it. And now this."

Maybe tomorrow; certainly not today. The registrar rambled on. "And that's not all. The office has been flooded with requests for transcripts from students transferring to other colleges. Like rats deserting a sinking ship."

Henry was numb. Only Charles O'Malley can save us now, he said to himself as he bade goodbye to the registrar.

This time he had no difficulty in reaching O'Malley. The receptionist put him through immediately.

"Doc? Chuck here. I understand you have a few problems. . . . Well, let's meet at the Afton for lunch tomorrow. You're free? Good, then. See you tomorrow."

Grace was seriously concerned about her husband. The stress he was under could kill him. She shuddered as she recalled Ray's funeral. The same thing could happen to Henry. Ray had always appeared to be in perfect health, and now he was gone.

She wished she could have talked her husband out of returning to academia. It made no sense. Since then he had
refused to go on vacations, except a day or two at a time, and
you could tell by looking at him that he took his worries with
him.

The media, which had been so supportive when Santa
Sophia was first started, added to the pressure by their nega-
tive reporting. Santa Sophia had changed from a noble experiment into a whipping boy. Obviously, somebody was
leaking stories to them. You can tell yourself you can ignore
it, but in reality you cannot.

At dinner that evening Grace served chicken Marengo, its
sauce deliciously flavored with onion, garlic, tomatoes, mush-
rooms, butter, tarragon and dry white wine.

"Delicious!" he said, although there was not enough pepper.

After a while, she added, "You know, dear, it would be
nice if we entertained your colleagues some time soon. We
didn't this Christmas time, you know."

He was slightly annoyed. Didn't she realize how much he
had on his mind these days? A dinner party for twelve guests
would require a lot of effort, and he didn't think he had any
to spare. On the other hand, it would be good to put his mind
to something other than trying to keep the college going. Yes,
why not do it?

"OK," he said, then he wished he hadn't. He suddenly
remembered that Ray Donato would not be there. Neither
would Ray's widow, Angela. Oh, she'd be invited, all right.
But experience had taught him that whenever he lost a friend

through death, that friend's surviving spouse always seemed to drift away, too. So make that ten guests; Ray and Angela would not be attending.

He hated to do it, but he'd force himself.

"What do you think we ought to serve?" he asked his wife.

His mind was already on the menu. Something unusual. Anybody could broil a steak and turn potato flakes into mashed potatoes. More was expected of an amateur Creole chef like Henry Boudreaux. What about ethnic preferences? There'd have to be compromises. Saul's wife had always served kosher food whenever they had dined in her home, but Saul made it clear that while they maintained a kosher house-hold, "When we dine out, anything goes."

"I can see you're already planning," his wife said, and "I think your menu will be even more elaborate than usual. But let me make one suggestion. Prepare the kinds of dishes you can freeze, so you're not under so much pressure. And we'll hire Hélène to clean up the next day."

TWENTY-ONE

Four days before the dinner, Grace sprained her ankle.
"Postpone the dinner," she urged her husband. "You can't do
all that work alone."

Henry didn't relish the idea, but neither was he willing to
cope with the problem a week or two away.

"I'll manage," he assured her. "I'll make the shrimp gumbo
today or tomorrow and freeze it. Of course, you can't do that
with jambalaya. Not without it losing a lot of its texture and
flavor. For dessert we'll cheat a little bit and buy French
pastries."

Grace was seated at the end of the table, her foot propped
up on a pillow, while Henry served the food. He was annoyed
that his frequent trips to the kitchen kept him out of most of
the conversation, but he did manage to pick up bits of the
talk.

. . .The concept of racial purity is an absurdity that has outlived its usefulness. . .

Better rinse off those gumbo dishes now, or you'll regret it in the morning.

. . .You're reading more out of my writings that I wrote into them — which is exactly what I intended. . .

Time to serve the jambalya; don't forget the trivet.

. . .No matter what dire situations people find themselves in, they usually manage to survive; some of them even manage to prosper. . .

. . .As amoral as a game of chess. . .

"How about another coke, Patricia? Paul?"

. . .Whoever said man is a rational being was only half right; he is half-rational and half-rationalizer . . .

. . .The market system which we recommend so highly to the Russians sounds good to me; we should try it. . .

. . .We all want to buy in a highly competitive market, but sell in one where competition is restricted. . . .

. . .In other words, we prefer to avoid the attrition of competition. . .

"Are you comfortable, Honey?"

*. . .A coward can get a medal for bravery if he works hard
enough at it. . . .*

*. . .Gresham's law of education: Bad teachers tend to destroy
the effectiveness of good teachers — or drive them out of the
profession. . .*

*. . .Holy Mother Church is a Jewish mother; she showers
upon her children tender loving care; then she refuses to let
them grow up. . .*

"Now how about some desert?"

. . . My enemies' enemies are my friends. . .

Henry sat alone at his table on the second floor of the
Afton Restaurant, impatiently awaiting the arrival of his tardy
host. He did not have to wait long before Charles O'Malley
entered the room and approached his table. A look of triumph
was on his face as he greeted Henry. After insincere greetings
on the part of both of them, Henry got down to business.

"Things are not going well, Chuck."

"Yes, I know."

"Graduate schools in the New York area seem to be stalling
in the cases of all but the most obviously competent applicants
among our graduates. Rumors of our approaching bankruptcy
are buzzing about the campus. What's worse, applications for
the next freshman class have fallen off drastically, and with
this trend our anticipated revenues for the next semester have
fallen below the break-even point. Without your continued
help, we'll be wiped out."

To Henry it felt like going to confession and revealing to the priest a very embarrassing sin.

For a long moment, they looked at each other in silence. Then O'Malley said, "Sorry, Doc. I'll have to foreclose on you. The Federal and State banking authorities would have my ass if I didn't. You see, your collateral is insufficient, all things considered."

Henry tan face became pale. "What!"

Chuck relished the moment of triumph. "Now I'm going to make it as easy as I can for you. Instead of going through the process of a foreclosure, and all the pain that would cause you and your faculty, I'm going to make an out-of-court settlement with you which will include a year's salary for all your senior professors. I'll also pick up all outstanding obligations of the now defunct Santa Sophia College so you won't have those headaches."

[Big of him, thought Henry. Or is it? No doubt he has an ulterior motive for buying the senior faculty off.]

Instead of revealing his thoughts by telling this con man off, he said calmly, "But what about the junior faculty? And over three hundred students?"

Evidently, Chuck did not regard this as a serious matter. "They're young. I'm sure they'll find something else. It's the old timers I'm concerned about. They have nowhere to go."

[How nice of you.]

"So I'll have my attorney draw up the paperwork. [He has probably already done so] and I'll see you next week.

"Don't worry, Doc. You'll come out of this smelling like a rose."

[Not if we do it your way, Chuck.] "Thanks, Chuck. You

know where to find me."

They shook hands as Chuck stood up.

"I gotta run now, Doc, but stick around and have a steak on me."

Henry smiled feebly. "Thanks, Chuck, but I'm really not hungry now."

"Well, suit yourself. I understand. *Adios*."

Henry smiled again. [Like hell you understand.]

As he drove home Henry almost admired Charles O'Malley. Those two congressional committees would never lay a hand on him; they were outclassed. He had done nothing illegal, yet he had done nothing honest. The only thing that stops a robber baron like Charles is another robber baron, just as crooked and a bit smarter. He probably had just bought himself a new borough council, and with it a new zoning committee. As soon as he acquired that campus, a simple resolution would grant him a variance which would at least quadruple the value of that piece of real estate. And the press would probably hail the move as bringing jobs and business into the town.

A zoning committee can manipulate the value of a piece of real estate within its jurisdiction by rezoning, or simply by granting a variance. Of course, those opposed can go to court and sometimes even win, but this is a lengthy, expensive procedure with no assurance of success. It's up to the opposition to prove that the committee is acting illegally.

Henry lacked the resources to go to court, so O'Malley's bank would soon own the grounds and buildings of Santa Sophia College. The aroma of the steak had been appetizing, and suddenly Henry was aware that he was hungry. But not that hungry.

Well, Joseph, I tried. God knows I tried. But it seems as if the relative density of SOB's has passed the point of toleration and is approaching the point of saturation. Again, maybe that's just old age speaking. Four years of hard work goes down the tubes and a rich man gets richer at my expense. There's nothing I can do about it. I guess subconsciously I knew it all along, didn't I? My noble experiment wiped out. Well, from now on it's my Social Security check and my TIAA pension. Nothing better to do than to work on my book again and wait for death. Oh well, there is something good to be said for that. Now that I no longer have big money at my disposal, everybody will ignore me, and leave me in peace.

TWENTY-TWO

Henry thought of April as lilac time, but the winter of 1993 lingered and it was not until mid-May when his lilacs bloomed. Suddenly he remembered that he had promised his daughter-in-law that he would baby-sit David. He had just returned home with the boy when the doorbell rang so insistently that David went to the door. Following him, his grandfather saw a red-faced Ernie Hause standing in the doorway. Not again, he thought, expecting more insults and threats. Then he became alarmed. There was something wild about Ernie, something even crazier than usual.

"Well, Boudreaux," he snarled, inviting himself in, "the time has come."

Relishing the terror he saw on Henry's face, he prolonged his own ecstasy.

"Yes, Boudreaux. I came here to kill you, but I've changed my mind."

Apparently contradicting himself, he drew a hand gun out

of his jacket pocket.

"Yes, I changed my mind now that I find your grandson here. I'm going to kill him instead. Right in front of you. Yes, Boudreaux, a grandson for a grandson. You murdered my grandson and I'm going to execute yours."

Instinctively, Henry got between Ernie and David and grabbed at the madman's handgun. The gun fired, and Henry felt the slug hit his belly. With a low growl, Max threw himself at Ernie, sinking his fangs into his wrist. Ernie howled, as he tore his bleeding wrist away from the dog. In his rage he poured shot after shot into the helpless animal. Feeling faint and losing consciousness fast, Henry saw that his grandson had moved to his right, exposed, helpless. Vaguely he heard the pistol click on an empty chamber just before he slugged Ernie below the belt with all his remaining strength as he passed out.

He regained consciousness in the ambulance. Ernie occupied the other stretcher. "David?" Henry asked the volunteer.

"He's all right, Dr. Boudreaux," the volunteer, a young neighbor, replied. He could not recall her name. "He's with the Laughneys next door, very much worried about his grandpa but otherwise OK. They also notified your wife."

His eyes began to focus until they made out the fuzzy form of a policeman he knew slightly.

"It's OK, Doc. Looks like you took pretty good care of him, so we're taking him to the hospital along with you. I'm here to make sure he doesn't recover suddenly and get away. According to Mrs. Laughney, it's a case of attempted murder. Not to mention that poor dog he killed."

That poor dog. Yes. Now he remembered. Max had saved

his life and he had been shot for it again and again. He
passed out a second time.

When Henry again regained consciousness, he was in the
recovery room of Morristown Memorial Hospital. His head
hurt so badly he didn't even notice the pain in his abdomen.

"You're going to be all right, Dr. Boudreaux," said a nurse
hovering above him. He assumed that she was a nurse, but
these days white uniforms were optional so you can never tell.

"Dr. McDonald removed the bullet. No complications.
Your wife and daughter-in-law are here. They'll be in to see
you, but only for a minute or two.

Later, in Room 344, surgical patients, they completed their
visit. He told them about Max's heroism. Reluctantly, Inez
told him how his beautiful dog had died before the Laughneys
could get him to his veterinarian. He already knew his dog
was dead. No dog could survive that many bullets fired at
point blank range. He hated Ernie with all his heart and soul.
He did not believe in capital punishment, but he wished Ernie
dead. Such shit should be flushed down the sewer. When he
told them about Ernie's attempt to kill not him but his grandson, Inez shuddered.

On the way out, Inez said to her mother-in-law, "We'll have
to get Dad another dog, another golden retriever."

"Yes," Grace agreed, "but not just yet."

A day later, when Henry was contemplating his past and
his future, a nurse asked him if he were up to seeing a report-
er from the Morristown Daily Record who wanted to do a
follow-up story on the shooting. He was. The interview also

included the story of Santa Sophia.

Tired by the brief interview, Henry had fallen into troubled sleep. He dreamed that Max was behind the wheel of his car, driving. He shouldn't be doing that, he thought; he has no driver's license. Then he saw Max sink his teeth into Ernie Hause's wrist. He shouldn't do that either. Unless — He saw his dog fall to the floor, his gushing blood reddening his golden coat. He awoke in a cold sweat.

Perhaps I should have done it, he thought. He had resolved to have Max put to sleep when he became helpless, and he was almost helpless. Where did that old dog find the strength to attack Ernie? He could no longer climb into the back seat of the Omni for the rides he loved so well, and he could barely make it up the back steps after his visits to the compost heap. It was only a matter of time, very little time. That's what a good master would do for a faithful animal. Put him to sleep. Too bad there was no one to do as much for the master.

But if Max had not been there, David would now be dead, and perhaps he would too. No, Max would not have wanted it that way.

The same day another visitor sneaked into his hospital room. Ernie's wife was there, entering under the pretense of visiting the husband who had already been discharged from the hospital only to be lodged in the Morris county jail.

Seeing her he expressed surprise that Ernie was still hospitalized. This she ignored.

"You really hurt him," she said. "You hit him below the belt, too. You could've killed him. But he's going to be all right."

So what's that to me, he asked himself.

"I'm sorry the way things turned out," she continued, "but they could have been much worse. Ernie was out of his mind since he lost his grandson, and you are a grandfather, Mr. Boudreaux, so you can understand that.

"You know, Mr. Boudreaux, Ernie didn't mean to harm you or your grandson. He only meant to scare you."

"Really?"

"Really. Ernie wouldn't harm a fly. Your vicious dog threw him off."

Max a vicious dog? Henry was getting angrier. "But he didn't mind pumping five bullets into the dog and one into me. And he would have killed a helpless, innocent child if there had been another bullet left in his gun. Really, Mrs. Hause, I can't buy that."

"But he was crazy. Crazy with grief. He didn't know what he was doing."

"He was there to kill me, and then decided to 'execute' my grandson. Execute, Mrs. Hause. No terrorist can execute a person. Only a government can execute. A terrorist like your husband can only murder."

"What will happen to him?"

"That will be decided in a court of law. He'll probably go to prison or to a mental institution."

"But not if you testified that it was an accident. The gun went off accidentally when you grabbed him."

"And the attempt to kill David with an empty gun?"

"You don't know that for sure. You were about to pass out, remember? Maybe you imagined it."

"I didn't imagine it. I know."

"But you could, as a good Christian, say you weren't certain. Give him the benefit of a doubt."

"Good Christians don't lie, Mrs. Hause, especially under oath. No, there is no doubt in my mind. No doubt at all. I am going to tell it as I saw it. Your attitude is rotten, lady. Now get out of here before I get a lot sicker than I am."

He need not have spoken. A nurse appeared and evicted the uninvited visitor.

"Bastard," she muttered, leaving. "You bastard." And down the corridor, more loudly, "You *educated* bastard!"

The nurse felt Henry's pulse and gave him a strong sedative while apologizing for her failure to intercept the intruder. Still it seemed like a long time before he fell asleep.

The first and only graduation day at Santa Sophia was on Saturday, May 29, 1993. Acting President Robert Chang presided. It was a cloudy and mild day, but too threatening to hold the ceremonies out of doors. The twenty-four young men and twenty-five young women assembled in the rear of the gymnasium-auditorium in caps and gowns and black hoods trimmed in white. The commencement address would be delivered by Brother Benedict, who remembered other graduations in that same auditorium when the weather was stifling hot. The forty-nine graduates who moved up the aisle to the taped sounds of *Pomp and Circumstance* were well aware that they would be the only graduates Santa Sophia would ever have, and they wondered how this would affect their future. Reassuring was the relatively high scores most of them had received in the Graduate Record Exams. They felt that they would have no difficulty getting into graduate schools.

Francis Nesbit, the salutatorian, began his address with the

self-confidence of a born orator.   Acting President, Dr.
Chang, tried to catch his words, but, from time to time, he
found his mind drifting back to events of the previous four
years. The times they were looking for ways to spend Joseph
White's money, the false starts, the hopes which proved false.
A loud audience reaction brought him back to the present.

". . . the two years and eight months I have spent at Santa
Sophia were the most fruitful in my life. I have not only
earned a college degree; I have received a liberal education. If
that sounds like tautology, I assure you it isn't.   I have not
only 'taken' eight semesters of Spanish; I have acquired a
fluency in Spanish. And I have learned to appreciate Hispanic
culture. I have not simply 'taken' eight semesters of English,
but, unlike certain million-dollars-a-year anchor persons on
TV, you'll never hear me say 'between you and I'. And I can
draw a recognizable map of the United States from memory
and correctly print in the names of all fifty states. I know I
should have learned all this in grade school, or at least in high
school, but how many of us do? Ask yourselves how many air
bubbles there are in your own education. Well, there are still
far too many in mine, but it's not Santa Sophia's fault. Daily
interaction with the faculty and students of this college has
burst many of them.

"Now if this seems like bragging, that's exactly what it is.
But I'm not bragging about myself and what I have achieved
but about my college and what it has achieved for me and for
forty-eight other young people like me. And there's more to
brag about. Apart from our academic studies, Santa Sophia,
which means holy wisdom, has taught us to respect the dignity
of labor. Each of us has been, at one time or another, a jani-

tor, a security guard, a cook, a gardener, a bookkeeper and a secretary. We have learned — and applied — word processing and data processing. We have learned how to tap the vast resources of knowledge locked up in distant data banks. We have learned how to broil a steak without burning it or drying it out. We have learned to live in the modern world."

Thunderous applause.

"I'm reminded of a story. It seems that during the Great Depression a young college graduate was forced to take a job in a factory. He was told by his foreman to take a broom and sweep the floor. 'But I am a college graduate,' he protested. The foreman replied, 'In that case, I'll show you how.' "

Laughter.

"Well, ladies and gentlemen, Santa Sophia has shown me how."

Now Robert was pretending to pay close attention to Brother Benedict's commencement address, but only pretending. His mind was on the man in a Morris county hospital with a bullet hole in his belly. Does anyone ever recover from a bullet hole? Really recover?

The good monk's words drifted in to interrupt his thoughts.

"Santa Sophia did not fail; it was conceived along sound educational principles. It was managed by competent and conscientious people. It had the support of students who were eager to learn. It did not fail. It was sabotaged by unscrupulous people whose only goal was acquisition, and whose only code of morality was the bottom line. . ."

Polite applause told Robert that the speaker had done his duty.

Dolores Pryer was the valedictorian. "During my solemn walk up to this platform," she was saying, "I heard a female chauvinist remark to the effect that the honor conferred on me proved that women are smarter than men."

Nervous laughter.

"It proves nothing of the kind."

Silence.

"Unlike at some other colleges, at Santa Sophia the honors were based solely upon the cumulative quality point scores. In the case of the two top honors, there was a difference in cume of approximately one one-hundredth of a point. Furthermore, seven other graduates had cumes which came within a tenth of a point of the highest. For most purposes, the differences are hardly worthy of notice.

"What these data do reveal, however, is that Santa Sophia was highly successful. . . ." Her voice cracked with emotion.

She broke into tears and could no longer continue.

The next day Henry awoke from his nap to find a young man seated in his room. What now? he thought.

"I didn't want to awaken you, Dr. Boudreaux, and I apologize for the intrusion, but I think you'll be glad I intruded. You see, sir, your experience will no doubt be of interest to my readers. I'm Clifford Moore, a feature writer for the Times. I'd like your permission to do an article on your recent experience. I think it would have a strong popular appeal, particular the boy and the dog elements. We'd pay you for your collaboration, of course."

Henry took a while to answer. "I'm not entirely awake Mr. — Moore, isn't it? But if I understand you, with my cooperation an article will appear in the Times. I'd like that very much, with a few provisions of my own."

Moore had expected as much. Usually, they want to know how much money is in for them. Henry had not mentioned money.

"I want to approve your final copy. I reserve the right to delete anything I disapprove of."

The writer hesitated. "Well, I don't know. But let's talk about it."

Henry talked. "In the first place, I want it understood and I want it emphasized that the concept of a no-frills college is sound. The bankruptcy of Santa Sophia was due to extraneous circumstances beyond our control."

"Sounds reasonable, if you are able to demonstrate it to the satisfaction of our editors."

"Secondly, the bullet I took in my gut had nothing to do with Santa Sophia. You must emphasize that point in your article."

"Anything else?"

"Yes. You have two themes here, a bankrupt college and an attempted murder. You must emphasize the former and minimize the latter, the shooting, in your story."

"Sounds reasonable enough," Moore said, apparently relieved that these were demands that he could live with. "Now do you mind if I use your phone to call my editor?"

TWENTY-THREE

A week later, Henry was back home, recuperating. For-
bidden by his doctors to exert himself in any way, he confined his activities to nothing more rigorous than reading,
writing and thinking. His first problem was how to minimize
the impact of O'Malley's heartless tactics on the stranded
students and professors.

The doorbell rang. At first he thought was another un-
wanted telephone call. It was his accountant, Saul's daughter,
Alicia. "My father wanted to come, but I wouldn't let him. I
know how it is when you two old cronies get together, and I
thought it might be hazardous to his health."

She had no way of knowing why her words made Henry
laugh until his incision hurt.

Making herself at home, Alicia put her leather attaché case
on the dining room table, and took two ledgers out of it.

"Two sets of books, Alicia? I thought that was illegal,"
Henry commented, still grinning.

"Not in this case. You see, Henry, this well-worn ledger is the true set, the one some people hide from the IRS, the one we show the IRS. The other represents what your ledger would have looked like if it had not been for the malicious maneuvers of a certain Charles O'Malley and his flunkies, notably Dennis Valez. What this second book, which I have authored, proves is that the whole idea of Santa Sophia is viable. It proves that, without O'Malley's manipulating things behind the scene, Santa Sophia would be alive and well and still doing business in New Jersey."

Henry was amazed.

"But you must have spent many hours authoring the second book," he finally said.

The woman was silent.

Henry could no longer hold back his tears. "That took so much effort, Alicia, and I don't know how I'm ever going to pay you. I no longer have a job and my pension and social security checks — "

You can't let a grown man cry, especially an elderly one.

"Forget it, Henry. Let's just say that a woman has to satisfy her curiosity. In my case, it was about my father. I never knew him to waste his time on anything, and Santa Sophia certainly looked like a waste of time to me when he first got involved."

Henry knew that was the truth, but it certainly was not the whole truth. And he loved her for it. She snapped her attaché case closed, kissed him on the top of his bald head, and said, "Get well soon."

Alicia's visit provided Henry with more food for thought. He realized that he had a lot of work ahead of him. Liquidating Saint Sophia. Then he realized that Chuck had chosen the ideal time to pull the rug out from under him — from Chuck's standpoint. Timing is essential in a case like this one. Finally, it occurred to him that if his adversary could use timing tactics to his advantage, so could he. The establishment of Santa Sophia was to O'Malley only a device to delay matters until the timing was ripe to grab another valuable piece of real estate at a bargain price. The people he hurt in the process did not matter to him.

Henry resolved to seek out O'Malley's enemies; my enemies' enemies are my friends. No doubt in this case he had many unknown friends. Why not start with the lawyers O'Malley must have alienated? His inquiries turned up the name of Edwin Knowles, an attorney who hated the very name of Charles O'Malley.

"Time is money to O'Malley," Knowles had said. "We'll make him pay dearly for that time. Refuse his 'generous' offer to settle out of court until he sweetens the pot considerably. Threaten to delay his taking over the *corpus delicti* that was once Santa Sophia College by dragging him through the courts, or until his enemies have time to regroup and once again manipulate the zoning laws against him. Or until he came to reasonable terms with Santa Sophia. The law is a two-edged sword. It cuts both ways. Right?"

"Right!"

TWENTY-FOUR

"**I don't think you should go.** Doctor McDonald said that you are not supposed to drive a car until next month."

Henry hated to cross his wife, especially when he knew she was right.

"I must," he replied, firmly, after hesitating.

She knew he was right.

"Then let me drive you."

He shook his head. That would not do.

Finally, exasperated, she gave in. "Well, at least take my car."

He was glad to. Omni — Latin for "all" — is a big name for a little car. Her 1992 Buick LeSabre was certainly a better car to drive than his Omni for a person just recovering from surgery.

"And promise me that you'll go by way of Route 46."

He promised.

He didn't like to drive on Route 80 anyway, and he avoided it whenever he could. It was too difficult for a slow person to enter, and there were too many eighteen-wheelers humming along at sixty or seventy, not to mention all those other motorists trying to pass them.

The day was pleasant. The sun was shining and it was very warm for October. He wondered about the theories concerning the earth warming up. From a strictly selfish point of view, it would be all right with him if New Jersey became as hot as Florida. He liked hot weather, and yet he did not want to relocate in Florida. But if Florida's climate relocated in New Jersey, he would not complain.

But why did he feel he had to make this trip? What did he expect to find? Five years ago, after he had sold his success-ful typesetting business, he had wanted to travel, but he soon found that he could not make travel a vocation. So, like most other retired professors, he had started to write a book, one which even he doubted would ever be published. He guessed he'd pick up the book where he left off. He had to do something meaningful with the rest of his life, otherwise he might as well die tomorrow.

He turned off Route 10 to Route 46 half an hour after he had started out, marveling at all the development which had taken place on Route 10 over the past few years. He drove through one familiar town after another, Netcong, Budd Lake, over the top of the hill overlooking Hackettstown and, in little more than a glance, taking in the spectacular view on his way down into Hackettstown.

Autumn leaves lingered on many trees, reluctant to join their fallen brothers below. The twisting highway followed the Pequest River, a winding stream which seemed much too small to justify being called a river. Now, careful. Approaching the junction of 46 and 80 is tricky for a solitary driver with no one to direct his turns. He could make the wrong turn and have to do a lot of backtracking.

Ignoring the impatient horn-tooters behind him, he slowly and carefully found his way through the interchange at the Delaware Water Gap. He had to remind himself to concentrate on his driving and not let himself be distracted by the scenery as he drove through what must be one of the most beautiful scenic routes in the country. Glancing up at the mountain on his left, he was pleased to find that there was no longer a billboard marring its beauty. The environmentalists had evidently won out over the advertisers. For the time being. Money always wins in the long run, and we're all the poorer for it.

The line of traffic approaching the toll gates of the bridge that crossed the Delaware River was long enough to remind him that he was still in New Jersey where you have to wait in line for everything. But today the line moved quickly. He had been told that the toll had increased from twenty-five cents to a dollar, but, although it costs a dollar to get into Pennsylvania, it costs nothing to get out.

The second exit for East Strausburg, he kept reminding himself as he stayed in the inner lane at a normal speed until he had reached the first exit. Then he moved to the outer lane of the highway, slowing down enough to force those behind to go around him, until he entered the next off-ramp.

In the town he stopped to examine the crude home-made map he had stapled to a page of his 1993 journal.

Now let's see. Three blocks in and a left turn. Go 4.5 miles on the secondary road. The house at the foot of the mountain with two tall spruce trees embracing a gravel driveway.

An elderly woman answered his ring.

She looked at him suspiciously, then seemed to be reassured by the expensive new Buick.

"I beg your pardon, ma'am," he said, "but four years ago this house belonged to a friend. He was killed when his garage caught fire with him in his car. I wonder if you'd mind if I looked around for old time's sake."

Her suspicions vanished.

"Not at all, sir. You'll probably find my husband out there somewhere."

The grounds had been kept in good condition. The owner must still be in good physical shape. The fire-blackened spot where the garage had stood had been replaced by a bed of flowers, few of which had survived the season's first heavy frost.

"Good afternoon, sir."

He turned. The owner was a man in his late seventies, or possibly his early eighties. His bare head was covered with an abundance of long white hair. His red and brown plaid shirt had to have a liner, or he would be wearing a coat at this temperature. He introduced himself as Joe Brubaker.

"My wife told me that you were here. Go right ahead. Be my guest."

The house stood at the bottom of a five-acre plot. Most of the land was too steep to build upon unless you enjoy mountain climbing. It overlooked a small lake which reflected the house and the steep hill behind it. It was the kind of view that a landscape painter would want to put on canvas.

It was not long before Henry, still weak from his surgery, stopped climbing and sat on a convenient stone to catch his breath. He looked over the lake as he told himself that Joseph certainly knew how to select a summer home. Yes, it was about seven years since he had roamed these hills with his friend. That was not counting the last visit here five years ago. There was something about Joseph that day in 1986. There was a calm about his demeanor. He was different from the impression you usually got of him, like a bomb waiting for an excuse to explode. They had walked their usual steep trails. The summer day was hot, and soon they were both puffing.

"I guess we're both getting too old for this kind of exercise," Joseph had said.

"I like it." Henry was not willing to admit that he was just as winded as Joseph.

"I'm glad you do," Joseph said, thinking his friend was referring to his mountain retreat. "It's yours."

Henry was flabbergasted. He knew that his friend was rich enough to make him the gift without feeling it. Then the thought occurred to him: Joseph loves this place.

"But you love this place," he protested.

"But I won't be around to enjoy it much longer, so I want you and Grace to have it."

Henry was shocked. "Cancer?" was he only thing he could say.

Joseph shook his head "no." The truth finally occurred to Henry; Joseph intended to kill himself.

He was furious. "Oh, no you don't you sonuvabitch. I spent the last thirty years keeping you alive, and I won't have you throw all that back in my face."

Joseph was touched. For a long time he did not reply. Finally, he said, "You will be well paid for your efforts, Henry. To show my gratitude, in my will I have named the Boudreauxs as my heirs. There'll be more than a million dollars in my estate, not counting this property."

Now it was Henry's time to be silent. When he turned to face his friend, there were tears in his eyes.

"No you don't, you sonuvabitch. I won't touch a penny from you if it means that you are going to take your own life. I don't care what you do with your money. You can give it all to charity as far as I'm concerned because that's exactly what I'm going to do if I inherit it from you this way. I can do without blood money, especially if it comes from my closest friend, my blood-brother, as my Indian ancestors would say. Better still, tear up that will and make out a new one, making sure that the name "Boudreaux" does not appear in it as an heir."

Joseph's face showed emotion for the first time since Henry had known him, but he did not weep. Long ago he had been deprived of his tears.

They spent the rest of the day fishing in the lake. Symbolically, it was Joseph who caught all the fish as Henry reeled in an empty line again and again.

"Since you caught all the fishes, it is only fair that I should clean and cook them," he said.

"*Fait donc.* I'm a poor cook anyway, and when I fillet a fish, I leave most of the flesh on the bones."

"I know. That's the real reason I want to do the cleaning and the cooking."

Henry scraped the scales off the fishes and chopped off their heads and their fins. He gutted them and coated them, Creole style, with cornmeal. Then he found three symmetrical stones, each about a foot square, and formed them into a broken circle. He built a fire in the center. Taking a frying pan and bacon fat from Joseph's kitchen, he pan-fried the fish over the burning twigs. Even though their bread was stale, they made delicious fish sandwiches.

After supper, Henry had called his wife to say that Joseph had invited him to stay for the night. She said that it was a good idea since he would not be subjected to the strain of driving home at night. They built a fire in the fieldstone fireplace, since the mountain air had become chilly. Seated near the blazing fire, they had resolved the world's problems, political, religious, philosophical, through half the night.

"If I had a million dollars, I could change the world, " Henry had said.

"No, you couldn't. You could make a little difference, perhaps, but only a little difference."

Now, years later, Henry had to agree with his dead friend; Joseph was a lot closer to the truth than he had been. A million dollars could do very little, especially if it had the opposition of someone with billions at his disposal.

The next morning, as Henry was leaving, Joseph told him that he was taking his advice. That Henry, by his gesture, had given a new meaning to his life, and that he would go on living, for a while anyway. That he would start up a foundation, capitalized at a million dollars, and whatever money it would subsequently earn. It would be used by Henry to benefit mankind, once Joseph had passed on. In the meantime, he'd do his best to convert that million dollars into two million dollars or maybe even more.

The old man, Mr. Brubaker, found him under that same tree. Another kindred spirit, Henry thought. He was invited to stay for dinner with the Brubakers.

The fish his hostess served was not pan-fried; it was baked with a delicious sauce. As daylight began to fade, they ate on the screened front porch, overlooking the lake. The mountain beyond concealed the setting sun. Henry commented, "When I drive through the mountains, the sun appears to set several times, only to rise again when I reach a mountain top. There must be a message in there somewhere."

They talked about the beauty of the place.

"I love it better here than any place I've ever lived in," Mr. Brubaker said, "and I've lived in eight places in my eighty-one years. But taking care of it is getting to be too much for me. It's about time for me to buy a condominium where the only thing I'd have to do is vacuum the carpet and wash the dishes."

Henry asked him if that meant he would consider selling his house.

"Yes, for the right price."

"Name your price."

"I'd have to sleep on it. Why don't you spend the night here and I'll let you know in the morning."

Grace thought it would be a good idea. Henry went to bed thinking about their new summer home. A summer home for him and Grace; a winter home for Junior and his family. They loved to ski and Camelback was only a short distance away. Almost immediately he fell asleep. The mountain air always did that to him.

The next morning the price of seventy-five thousand dollars was quoted. Henry agreed without haggling, and gave him a check for a thousand dollars as a binder. He said he'd have the rest of the money within a week. Mr. Brubaker said that meanwhile he'd get all the legal formalities started.

An hour later Henry, contented, drove eastward on Route 80 into the glare of the morning sun.

Henry Boudreaux, President
Santa Sophia College
Eunice, NJ 07941

September 18, 1993

Mr. Edwin Knowles, Esq.,
Knowles, Batchelor and Potter
Attorneys-at-Law
297 Madison Avenue
Morristown, NJ 07960

Dear Mr. Knowles:

Thank you for your letter of September 11th. Sorry I missed your telephone call.

After consultation with our Board of Trustees, I am prepared to accept Mr. Charles O'Malley's offer to settle out of court as you recommended. As I understand it, each full professor will receive two years' salary after the closing of Santa Sophia. Each instructor will receive two years' salary plus a rent allowance of $1,000 a month for two years, and each of the matriculated students will have his tuition and fees paid until his graduation at a college of his choice in the State of New Jersey

It is also my understanding that Charles O'Malley will pay all legal costs involved in this transaction.

Thank you for the manner in which you have handled this matter.

Cordially,

Henry Boudreaux, Jr.

Dr. Henry Boudreaux
9 Spruce Street
Eunice, NJ 07940

October 12, 1993

Dr. J. Franklin Forbes, President
Cathay-Jones College
Fort Lauderdale, FL 34284

Dear Dr. Forbes:

Thank you for your letter of October 7th. I shall be happy to fly down to Florida and spend five days with you in consultation with regard to money-saving methods you might employ in the management of your institution. However, due to our many previous commitments, my services and those of my wife, who acts as my secretary, will not be available until the week of January 22, 1994.

Our terms are two first class round trip airline tickets to the airport most convenient to Fort Lauderdale, a suite in your best local hotel, meals in a good restaurant, and necessary transportation to and from the airports and while we are in Florida.

If this meets with your approval, please let us know within ten days. You will pay no consulting fee. This has already been paid by the late Dr. Joseph White.

Cordially,

Consultant